D0225522

Knowledge in Motion

Knowledge, Identity and School Life Series

Editors: Professor Philip Wexler, Graduate School of Education and
             Human Development, University of Rochester, New York,
             NY 14627, USA and
             Professor Ivor Goodson, Faculty of Education, University of
             Western Ontario, Canada.

Knowledge, Identity and School Life Series: 2

Knowledge in Motion:
Space, Time and Curriculum in Undergraduate Physics and Management

Jan Nespor

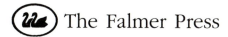 The Falmer Press

(A member of the Taylor & Francis Group)
London • Washington, D.C.

UK The Falmer Press, 4 John Street, London WC1N 2ET
USA The Falmer Press, Taylor & Francis Inc., 1900 Frost Road, Suite 101, Bristol, PA 19007

First published in 1994

A catalogue record for this book is available from the British Library

Library of Congress Cataloging-in-Publication Data are available on request

ISBN 0 7507 0270 2 Cased
ISBN 0 7507 0271 1 Paper

Jacket design by Caroline Archer

Typeset in 10/12pt Garamond by
Graphicraft Typesetters Ltd., Hong Kong.

Printed in Great Britain by Burgess Science Press, Basingstoke on paper which has a specified pH value on final paper manufacture of not less than 7.5 and is therefore 'acid free'.

Contents

Contents

Acknowledgments

The fieldwork for this study was made possible by a Spencer Postdoctoral Fellowship from the National Academy of Education. The arguments presented here do not necessarily represent those of the National Academy of Education and no endorsement is implied.

I am deeply grateful to a number of people who have helped me with this project over the years. Prior to and during the fieldwork period, Doug Foley and Gideon Sjoberg gave me wise counsel and moral support. Ian Westbury encouraged and supported my early attempts to write about the study. Later, as I was working on this book, my writing group of Judy Barylske, Liz Barber and Joyce Graham helped me try to straighten up the ideas that eventually became the first chapter. Jim Garrison read earlier versions of the first chapter and the chapters on physics and posed many helpful questions. Liz Barber gave a close critical reading to drafts of the entire book. Finally, Philip Wexler helped me through some key final revisions of the text. None of these people is responsible for the errors and problems that remain in the text. This book is dedicated to my mother.

Introduction

This book is the product of ethnographic fieldwork I did from June, 1986 to July, 1987 at a large public university — it enrolled some 36,000 undergraduates in the fall of 1986 — in the United States.[1] Parts of that fieldwork have been assembled here,[2] mixed up with traces of some of the reading I've done, and shaped into a story about the university's undergraduate physics and management programs.[3]

I've written about those programs because they're areas where education and power come together in crucial ways. Physics and management are disciplines deeply implicated in the domination of the physical and social worlds. The fact that both regulate membership and participation in their realms through educational requirements makes them prime areas for exploring how students get connected to core disciplines of modern society, and how they become parts of durable and extensive networks of power.

To address these issues, I'll argue, it will be necessary to rethink what it means to 'learn' or 'have' knowledge. I will propose that we shift our focus from individual minds and groups in face-to-face interaction, to questions of how activities are organized across space and time, and how organizations of space and time are produced in social practice.

I will treat the physics and management programs I studied not as exemplary cases of such programs, but as 'points of entry' (Smith, 1987) that give us access to the larger processes that constitute and reproduce disciplines. Those processes, I'll argue, center around the incorporation of students into discipline-specific temporal and spatial organizations of knowledge.

To talk about 'knowledge' and 'learning' in such terms I have patched together the theoretical language laid out in the first chapter. From psychological anthropology (e.g., Lave, 1988) I take the notion of knowledge and learning as products of social activity rather than isolated minds. From social studies of science (e.g., Latour, 1987) I borrow a way of talking about such knowledge-constitutive activities as organized by networks spread across space and time. Finally, from geography (e.g., Gregory, 1994) I take tools for understanding how such networks are organized, stabilized, maintained, and integrated into larger flows of cultural and economic action.

The result is not a complete or particularly supple language, and I take much comfort in Stuart Hall's (1992) suggestion that 'the only theory worth having is that which you have to fight off, not that which you speak with profound fluency' (p. 280; cf. Said, 1983). I have tried not to shift the burden of my struggles and inarticulateness onto the readers, but some may find the first chapter hard going. Those unacquainted with the ideas I am reworking may be bothered by unfamiliar terms and assumptions woven through the argument. Other readers, those who *are* familiar with some of the schools of theory from which I borrow, may be bothered by the way I pick out concepts and ideas from widely separated disciplines and re-shape them to fit my purposes: the way I place others' ideas, place them in strange juxtapositions, use them to address different questions than their authors imagined, and so forth. In Culler's (1983) sense, the first chapter clearly qualifies as 'theory':

> 'Theory' is a genre because of the way its works function . . . [to] exceed the disciplinary framework within which they would normally be evaluated and which would help to identify their solid contributions to knowledge. To put it another way, what distinguishes the members of this genre is their ability to function not as demonstrations within the parameters of a discipline but as redescriptions that challenge disciplinary boundaries (Culler, 1983, p. 9; quoted in Gregory, 1994, p. 10).

However, I do not intend that the chapter should be read as the theory for which the remainder of the book functions as illustration. The first chapter and the four that follow it are more like two ways of talking about the same issues. Jumping ahead in the argument I could say that the first chapter is more 'mobile' than the second: theories are ways of talking about worlds that can be moved about and used in different situations for different purposes. Theory does not subsume or explain 'empirical' work, it's simply a way of moving it, or as Latour (1988) suggests, of connecting different networks of knowledge-work:

> Theories are never found alone, just as in open country there are no clover leaf intersections without freeways to connect and redirect. . . . When a series of locations has been mastered and joined together in a network, it is possible to move from one place to another without noticing the work that links them together. *One* location seems 'potentially' to contain all the others. I am happy to call the jargon used to get by inside these networks 'theory', as long as it is understood that this is like the signposts and labels that we use to find our *way back*. . . . What we call 'theory' is no more and no less real than a subway map in the subway (pp. 178, 220).

Inasmuch as the first chapter introduces some of the terminology used in the later chapters you should read it first, just as you might read a map before getting on a subway train. But the program descriptions are not mere blow-ups or details of some 'total picture' contained in the first chapter. Instead, the remaining chapters focus on how the programs spatially and temporally organized the material practices of their students, and on how students in the programs began to be engaged in discipline-linked practices for producing spatial and temporal relations.

At the core, my argument is that learning is not an internal psychological process (so you won't see me trying to reconstruct the psychologies of individual students), but neither is it a product of activities in face-to-face interaction. The first part of this statement is a familiar point, made in various ways by Vygotskians, students of 'situated learning', and others. It's the second half of the statement that may generate some initial confusion, for what I'm going to argue is that 'face-to-face' interaction in specific situations *is never just that*, and that instead what we think of as 'interactions' and 'situations' are, as Doreen Massey (1993) puts it, 'articulated moments in networks of social relations and understandings' in which our 'experiences and understandings are actually constructed on a far larger scale than what we happen to define for that moment as the place itself, whether that be a street, a region or even a continent' (pp. 65–66).

On the one hand social activity is now stretched across vast expanses of space and time so that, for example, physics students in different parts of the United States engage in generalized social relations with one another and with faculty (defined, for example, by a standardized curriculum and routed through distant sites by textbooks, tests, and so forth), and compete with one another for positions in an academic network to which they all belong. This 'distanciation' of social action, as Anthony Giddens (1981) calls it, directs us to look at the 'face-to-face interactions' of students and faculty within a particular program, as accomplished through participation in networks of social relations that extend far beyond the program.

On the other hand, we can also talk, as Massey did, of all the spatially and temporally distant flows of activity intersecting within a given setting. This is what David Harvey (1989) refers to as 'time-space compression': the articulation of 'global' processes in 'local' settings (making that very distinction problematic), the sense in which physicists from Berkeley are closer in space-time to their colleagues in Europe than to migrant workers in the next county, or managers in New York to their counterparts in Tokyo than the poor in the South Bronx.

What this boils down to is the idea that when we act we're simultaneously interacting with the people and things in the immediate environment *and* with people and things spatially and temporally removed from us, but none the less present in the situation in some way. To understand how activity is connected to learning and knowledge we have to deal with *both* threads of interaction. This requires us to look closely at how distant activity is transported into and made manifest in particular settings, and at how activities in *those* settings are connected to activities and spaces elsewhere. These are the tasks that occupy most of my attention in the book, and if I have slighted other important issues it is because I have been overwhelmed with the complexity of the issues surrounding the material organization of local educational space-times and their integration, through specific representational technologies, with distant space-times of disciplinary practice.

The first program I discuss is physics. Chapter 2 examines how the program zoned students' activities into a small set of material and social spaces and compressed their time to foster the development of exclusive, within-program social ties. This produced a distinctive form of social organization organized around the practice of problem-solving. Chapter 3 develops an account of problem-solving as a way of integrating students into the discipline's way of organizing the world through textual representations. I show how the different components of the physics curriculum (e.g., textbooks, lectures, study activities) were tied together through representational technologies, and how students learned to 'move' and organize themselves within the textual systems of space and time constituted by those representational technologies.

Chapters 4 and 5 deal with a very different system for organizing people and practices and linking them with networks of power: the management program. I highlight the contrasts between the two programs when I can, but given the programmatic differences these chapters do not exactly parallel the chapters on physics. Instead, chapter 4 shows how the management program fragmented academic space-time and organized it into distinct, bounded, short-term units. In sharp contrast to the physics program, which strove to reorganize the world in terms of the academic discipline, the management program created (or at least reinforced) a sharp division between the school world and the business world. In chapter 5, however, I show how non-academic portions of the program nevertheless created lines of connection between the program and the business world by 'mobilizing' students in distinctive systems of material bodily practice.

The final chapter is a reflective commentary on major themes of the book and a look beyond it. I am conscious of the fact that since my fieldwork the proliferation of computer networks and on-line communications, especially in fields such as physics and management, may have substantially altered the configurations of the space-time networks I studied. The representational technologies I identify as mobilizing educational experience to fields of practice in the two disciplines may have changed radically. Any such changes, however, by making the distanciation and space-time compression of the fields more manifest, make a stronger case for the kind of analysis and theoretical language I am proposing here. This work is a beginning, an initial and incomplete exploration of a fluid terrain.

Notes

1 In the category system used in the university's official statistics, 76 per cent of the students were 'white', 9 per cent were 'Hispanic', 5 per cent were 'black', 4 per cent were 'Asian-American', and 7 per cent were foreign. In the university as a whole 54

per cent of the students were male, 46 per cent female. In the management program the male/female ratio was 1:1, but in physics men outnumbered women 9:1.

2 I didn't study 'the university' as a whole, nor did I 'observe' or 'participate in' every facet of undergraduate physics and management education. My focus was primarily on the academic side of student experience (although 'academic' and 'social' life often blurred). In the portions of the fieldwork dealing with physics and management, I conducted 51 taped interviews with students and faculty; observed many dozens of class sessions and study sessions; collected and analyzed course syllabuses, catalogs, textbooks, and students' classnotes; analyzed the transcripts of recent graduates in the fields; and 'hung out' with and talked informally with students outside the classroom.

3 There were 220 and 136 'officially declared majors' in physics and management respectively, putting them in the bottom third in size among undergraduate programs (the largest had well over 1,000 majors). All of these numbers, however, are unreliable. There were, first of all, inconsistencies I could never account for (variances up to 10 per cent) across the enrolment and 'declared majors' data that I received from three sources: the registrar's office, the institutional research office, and the departments themselves. Second, the number of management majors is artificially low because the business school doesn't allow students to 'declare' until their third years (though many decide earlier). Thus the physics number includes freshmen through to seniors, the management number only juniors and seniors. This inflates the numbers in physics, since freshmen and sophomores are systematically weeded-out. The physics numbers also mislead by compressing into the 'senior' category all students who have been in the program more than three years. Since only 5 per cent of those who graduate from the program do so in four years this category actually includes several different age cohorts.

Chapter 1

Knowledge in Space and Time

Most forms of social theory have failed to take seriously enough not only the temporality of social conduct but also its spatial attributes. At first sight, nothing seems more banal and uninstructive than to assert that social activity occurs in time and space. But neither time nor space have been incorporated into the center of social theory, they are ordinarily treated more as 'environments' in which social conduct is enacted . . . rather than [as] integral to its occurence (Giddens, 1979, p. 202; quoted in Soja, 1985, p. 120).

My strategy in this chapter will be to dismantle a network of assumptions about 'knowledge' and 'learning' by depicting educational practice and research as revolving around a simple question: how is activity in one setting (such as a classroom) related to activity in settings distant in space and time (other classrooms or workplaces)? I want to suggest that all our notions of learning, development, teaching, curriculum and reproduction can be read as answers to this question about space-time relations, yet all suppress considerations of spatiality. At one extreme we have information processors and cognitive structures that roam unproblematically across space-time, at the other situated or distributed cognitions that don't move at all (and in between ideas that share the weaknesses of both). None of this will do. There are no disembodied heads about, but neither are there isolated social interactions or localized communities of practice. We live in a global world system and no analysis of knowledge and learning will suffice that cannot take this into account: that my activity writing this and yours in reading it cannot be explicated without understanding how we're linked to one another, to those around us, to world economies and global flows of culture that shape and provide resources for everyday practice.

The tactic of this work is to foreground the production and organization of space and time and look at schooling as a web of movements spun from multiple flows of material resources and representations. The focus is undergraduate education in the fields of physics and management. The topic is the production of actors for the spatial and temporal networks of power that we call disciplines.

In this chapter I construct a language for talking about how educational programs define trajectories[1] through material spaces — buildings, classrooms and laboratories — to bring students into contact with representations of other spaces and times — textbooks, equations, lectures, lab equipment, and so on — that make those 'absent' spaces 'present' in textual form. It is in these organizations of space and time that we will find the key to understanding how students 'learn' in fields of 'knowledge' such as undergraduate physics and management.

The substantive material of the book, then, focuses on students' academic encounters with the powerful disciplines they aspire to belong to, but the thread that ties the material together is the issue of how education is accomplished as a space-time process. The best place to begin addressing that issue is an arena from which space and time have usually been thoroughly excluded: the 'individual mind', the processes of cognition and learning.

From Individual 'Learners' to Networks of Knowledge Builders

Over the past quarter of a century 'learning' has commonly been conceived as a process taking place within individuals. People were said to gradually build up integrated capacities — composed of 'attitudes', 'rules', 'schemata', 'domain knowledge', 'contextual modules', or whatever — that could be carried around, called up, and deployed as needed in specific contexts (LCHC, 1982, p. 651). Contexts themselves were usually conceptualized in terms of decontextualized 'problems' or 'tasks' (e.g., Lesgold, 1988; cf. McDermott, 1990; Larkin, 1985, for physics; Isenberg, 1987, for management). Since the focus was usually on the individual's mental representations of the tasks, the effect, as Lave (1988) points out in her powerful critique of cognitive science, was a reduction of the social world to representations in individual minds.

This focus on discrete, independent individuals has been shared by approaches as dissimilar as the social psychological accounts that focused on individuals' attitudes and orientations (Perry, 1970; Katchadorian and Boli, 1985), and the cognitive psychologies that formulated 'learning theory' in terms of the internal architecture of 'the learner' (e.g., 'Conspicuous in the basic equipment of the learner is a memory system of virtually unlimited capacity . . .' etc., Estes, 1989, p. 42). In all of these approaches considerations of space and time were suppressed: the 'individuals' studied were not situated in specific social-historical fields of practice, and the 'tasks' the individuals engaged in were considered as bounded, homogeneous events rather than intersections of multiple on-going activities.[2]

To begin re-inserting space and time into accounts of educational practice we have to let go of 'the individual' and look for units of analysis that can be spatially and temporally situated. As Butler (1988) and Kondo (1990) argue, the preoccupation with 'individuals' is grounded in a 'metaphysics of substance' that creates a rigid division between the 'psychological' and the 'social'.

Identities are, in this view, fixed, bounded entities containing some essence or substance that is expressed in distinctive attributes. This conventional trope opposes 'the self' as bounded essence, filled with 'real feelings' and identity to a 'world' or to a 'society' which is spatially and ontologically distinct from the self (Butler, 1988). Indeed, the academic division of labor recapitulates this distinction in its separation of the disciplines, distinguishing 'psychology' from 'sociology' (Kondo, 1990, pp. 33–34).

Getting around these dichotomies to a vision of actors as something more than mere sociological or psychological entities (or some additive combination of the two) is enormously difficult. Consider work in the tradition of Vygotsky (1978; 1986), where psychological processes are seen as inextricably linked to social activity. Newman (1990), for example, defines cognition as a property not of individual students but of the 'interactional systems' in which students engage (cf. also LCHC, 1982; 1983; Moll, 1990; Newman, Griffin and Cole, 1989; Wertsch, 1985):

What is outside the head is just as much a part of the cognitive system as what is inside the head. . . . Tasks and understanding are observed first in interaction before being internalized as an individual's capacity. . . . Meaning is actively constructed in interaction (Newman, 1990, p. 188).

Instead of mere carriers of mental 'substances', people — at least at certain points of time — are viewed as components of social-cognitive configurations. Instead of solving externally imposed tasks and problems they actively construct and resolve practical dilemmas. Their 'knowing' (although it ultimately takes the form of decontextualized, 'internal' essences) is the *product* of activities contextualized in space and time.

Consider how these ideas might reshape the way we talk about knowledge and learning: the way I make meaning when I'm sitting in the local bar arguing with someone about knowledge is different from how I make it right now as I'm writing this. In the bar meaning is constructed in conversation and it varies according to whom I'm talking, our level of sobriety and so forth. In my office I can consult books, articles, fieldnotes, interview transcripts and earlier drafts of this text. The difference between what I 'know' in the two settings isn't in my ability to articulate some head-knowledge that remains constant across settings, nor do the books, people, or other elements of the contexts simply 'add to' some knowledge that already exists in my head. Rather, in the two settings I'm part of different cognitive systems (I'm a different 'I'). My 'psychological' state is integrally connected to, indeed is a product of, my 'social' situation (which includes inanimate 'tools' as well as other people). Finally, my experiences in each setting alter me, my individual mind, in some durable way (I internalize something) that shapes future activity.

The problem with this approach is that it depicts the social distribution of knowledge and 'cognition' as a transitory or intermediary stage on the route to 'internalized' — that is, despatialized and detemporalized — knowledge (cf. Lave and Wenger, 1991). In this sense, Vygotskian work moves 'cognition' back and forth from one side of the social-psychological divide to the other but fails to challenge the system of representation that creates 'the social' and 'the psychological' as opposed categories in the first place.[3] More importantly, even on their own terms, Vygotskian approaches succeed in integrating the social and the psychological only by embracing an extremely narrow conception of 'the social'. In practice they focus on face-to-face interactions taking place in small, circumscribed settings. Absent are considerations of social structural or systemic properties, of interactions between people and things that are *distant* from one another.[4] What makes this neglect so problematic is that social organization itself, at least since the development of the modern world system, has expanded beyond immediate, face-to-face interactions to link the activities of individuals who may never be physically co-present or engaged in direct interaction with one another (Giddens, 1981). As Gregory (1988) puts it:

> Insofar as routinized social practices are recognizably the same over varying spans of time and space . . . they flow from and fold back into structural relations which reach beyond the 'here and now' to define *interactions with others who are absent in time or space.* This is what 'society' came to mean after the eighteenth century: the larger world stretching away from the human body and the human being (pp. 80–82; emphasis added).

Making sense of knowledge practice as 'interaction' with others distant in time and space — a form of interaction pervasive in modern society — is the key problem I'm working with in this book. People don't participate as 'individuals' in pristine or local small-scale 'communities of practice' (Lave and Wenger, 1991), nor do they take on stable 'indentities' by becoming 'full participants' in such communities. Such views ignore the fact that 'communities' aren't just situated *in* space and time, they are ways of *producing and organizing* space and time and setting up patterns of movement across space-time: they are networks of power. People don't simply move into these networks in an apprenticeship mode, they are defined, enrolled and mobilized along particular trajectories that move them across places in a network and allow them to move other parts of the world into that network. A 'community', if we still wanted to use the term, would have to be seen as composed of extremely heterogeneous and dispersed elements linked together in what, following Callon (1986), I will call 'actor-networks': fluid and contested definitions of identities and alliances that are simultaneously frameworks of power.

I will discuss these notions in the next section, but here let me try to give you a sense of what I'm talking about by reworking that account I gave above about my own 'cognitive system'. Before, I was worried about whether 'I' had

9

the same mind in the office as in the bar. But where am 'I' right now?[5] You and I, as reader and writer, are separated from each other in time and space, and move together now only through the medium of this text. The text describes people, places, and events — undergraduate programs of education in physics and management — that are spatially and temporally distant from both of us. Our relationship to them is different. You were never in the space-times of these programs, I was. Unlike the faculty and students who lived through the programs, however, I intersected with them only briefly — on the trajectory of a social science career — and now, instead of moving *through* them, I *move* them across time and distance and into your field of vision. I mobilize compressed, stabilized representations of them — fieldnotes and interview transcripts — and link them with other mobile representations ('the literature') to formulate this even more compressed and mobile account, a book. Times and spaces long gone now appear before your eyes. Read the text and there 'they' are. Does the text 'describe' them? It *creates* them, *constitutes* them (and me), not as fixed essences — the students or professors could create accounts to contest mine, or you could attack my technology for building and moving representations (my methodology) — but as the 'contestable and constrained stories' (Haraway, 1989) of a 'positioned subject' (Rosaldo, 1989). The fate of the stories is in the hands of others. To move them I need access to technologies and organizational means for circulating representations (publishers, distributors), and ultimately I need people like you to use my representations in your representations, in other times and spaces. To get access to these sorts of things, to spread myself out over space-time, I need a disciplinary apparatus.[6]

The 'knowledge' in this example isn't the property of a 'cognitive system' (whether conceived as intra- or inter-psychological in nature). Rather, to borrow language from Callon (1986) and Latour (1987), it's the property of a network that produces space and time by mobilizing and accumulating distant settings in central positions: not just my own mobilizations of the programs, but the other mobilizations (the published theories and related studies in the literature) that I attach them to, the networks that connect us, and so forth. As Latour (1987) puts it:

> What is called 'knowledge' cannot be defined without understanding what *gaining* knowledge means. . . . 'Knowledge' is not something that could be described by itself or by opposition to 'ignorance' or to 'belief', but only by considering a whole cycle of accumulation: how to bring things back to a place for someone to see it for the first time so that others might be sent again to bring other things back. How to be familiar with things, people and events, which are *distant* (1987, p. 220).[7]

'Disciplines' such as physics and management are constituted by cycles of accumulation within networks that organize flows of people and things through space and time. I will treat education in physics and management as similarly being network/networking phenomena: as spatializing and temporalizing the activity of students to connect them to disciplinary practice. 'Learning' (in) a discipline isn't a matter of transforming one's psychological make-up (whether we see this as a function of developing internal 'equipment' or as the outcome of social activity). Instead, 'learning' should refer to changes in the spatial and temporal organization of the distributed actors/networks that we're always part of. It isn't, contrary to Vygotskian interpretations, that we move from social to 'internalized' knowing, from inter- to intra-psychological experiences: knowing is always distributed (Lave, 1988). Rather, we move through different spatio-temporal distributions of knowing. Students enter into disciplinary practices when they begin to move along trajectories that keep them within the narrow range of space-times and distributions that constitute the discipline: when they're physically mobilized through networks of physical settings, and when they begin to construct worlds through discipline-based systems of representation.

The effects of schooling depend on the spatial and temporal trajectories along which students are moving before and after educational encounters. Disciplinary education depends on the students moving along trajectories that keep them in contact with disciplinary networks. People need labs, notebooks, computers, equations, and colleagues to be 'physicists'; suits, offices, memoranda and organizations to be 'managers' (and the whole pathway that leads people into configurations with these elements is the key here, not mere possession of them). Drop a student or a physicist or a manager on a deserted island without their tools and colleagues and the questions of what they 'know' and in what sense they've 'learned' are rendered moot. Since learning and knowledge are not properties of individual actors we cannot speak of someone having 'learned' differential equations or financial ratios unless they're moving along a trajectory that at least periodically re-assembles the distributed or networked actor in practice-relevant configurations.

Networks and Actor-Networks

Let me try to clarify some of the ideas just introduced. 'Network' is an ambiguous concept, but a basic definition points to spatially dispersed elements that have been linked together over time. The linkages connecting networked elements are as important as the nature of the elements themselves. As Latour (1987) points out:

> The word network indicates that resources are concentrated in a few places — the knots and the nodes — which are connected with one another — the links and the mesh: these connections transform the scattered resources into a net (p. 180).

The content of the networked elements and the structure of the ties connecting them are not fixed and static (cf. Powell, 1990; Perrucci and Potter, 1989; Wellman, 1983). Networks expand, contract, and shift configuration over time, and even the most stable and predictable of them are constantly being reappropriated and redefined by the nature of the flows that animate them (just as a driver's route — and what he or she transports — may vary from day to day through a relatively stable system of roadways). Understanding those flows, however, isn't just a matter of understanding 'individual' trajectories (a particular driver's needs or desires or skills), but of understanding the ongoing social activities that enmesh the entire network (the social and economic forces that shape a society of drivers).

What I'm insisting on is that we push our analysis of the distributed actors we study — the links and mesh of the networks we trace — further back and out in space and time from our 'point of entry': further, certainly, than I'm able to manage in later chapters. No 'psychology' of 'learning' will be acceptable that isn't also a political economy of knowledge.

Before sketching the outlines of such a framework, however, I want to consider briefly a compelling alternative to the 'network' orientation, Lave and Wenger's (1991) conception of learning as legitimate peripheral performance in 'communities of practice'.

There is much to admire in this work: it rejects the preoccupation with 'internalization' that plagues Vygotskian approaches, and instead focuses on learning as a facet of social practice, as part of a process of acquiring an identity in a community of practitioners. The problem is that these (human) communities are treated as bounded, strictly local settings seemingly unconnected and unconnectable to other spaces and times. People move in or out of Lave and Wenger's circumscribed version of the 'social world' in terms of participation (although no attention is given to the trajectories that bring people to the peripheries of particular communities in the first place), but the question of how such communities are structured, maintained and connected to one another across space and time cannot be asked within the assumptions of the framework. In a sense, in spite of rejecting many of the core assumptions of traditional psychologies, Lave and Wenger remain locked into the *standpoint* of psychology — the focus on the 'individual' (not necessarily a person, but a bounded, local entity) developing through the peculiar, despatialized time of psychology. Where their focus is on understanding how one gets to be at home on isolated islands of practice, mine is on movement through the dense strands of practices that hold together worlds of knowledge.

What I am searching for is a way of talking about how people move into (become enmeshed in) fields of practice understood as organizations of and ways of producing activities, spaces, and times. Callon's (1986; 1987) 'actor-network' theory is the primary resource I draw on. Actor-network theory portrays activity in terms of the efforts of an explicitly distributed and spatialized network of entities whose linkages to one another are ongoing accomplishments:

The actor-network is reducible neither to an actor alone nor to a network. Like networks it is composed of a series of heterogeneous elements, animate and inanimate, that have been linked to one another for a certain period of time. . . . But the actor-network should not, on the other hand, be confused with a network linking in some predictable fashion elements that are perfectly well defined and stable, for the entities it is composed of, whether natural or social, could at any moment redefine their identity and mutual relationships in some new way and bring new elements into the network. An actor-network is simultaneously an actor whose activity is networking heterogeneous elements and a network that is able to redefine and transform what it is made of (1987, p. 93).

The principal virtue of this framework is that it allows us to look at identity and practice as functions of ongoing interactions with distant elements (animate and inanimate) of networks that have been moblized along intersecting trajectories. Lave and Wenger (1991) provide a foil again: their masking of the wider social world makes problematic their equation of 'learning' with 'acquiring an identity' *within* a community. Identities crystallize in the tensions and pressures produced as different communities or actor-networks clash. Identities are shifting, contested stakes of networking practices that seek to produce or maintain a certain configuration of social space by excluding or restricting some people and things from participation while recruiting and reconstructing others to fit into the network.

Callon (1987) provides a useful terminology (albeit an awkward one in English) for describing how identities and alliances are forged through the self-constitutive activities of actor-networks. Actor-networks such as physics and management ('disciplines' for short) constitute themselves in part through educational practices that shape and sort would-be participants and organize their participation in disciplinary productions of space and time. Callon (1986) suggests that there are four 'moments' — not sequential stages of the process but overlapping aspects of the strategies and tactics of network builders — of this networking process: *problematization, interessement, enrolment,* and *mobilization.*

Problematization refers to the ways network builders (for purposes of exposition, the 'physics' and 'management' programs, although who's building what network is a question explored in the body of the text) define allowable identities and interests for people such as students (or for other actors such as organizations, etc.). The only appropriate identity for a student in the physics program, for example, was that of 'physicist-in-the-making' en route to a career in research. The program had defined itself as an 'obligatory passage point' along this trajectory — a space-time intersection that students had to move through to accomplish the defined identities and interests (Callon, 1986, pp. 204, 206).

Problematization isn't unproblematic, however. Students have to be detached from the networks to which they already belong and within which their identities have been defined, and there are other actor-networks in the university setting busy trying to impose different identities. Interessement refers to the strategies network builders use 'to impose and stabilize the identity of the other actors it defines through its problematization' (Callon, 1986, p. 207), and the key to this process is the creation of barriers that can be placed between the entities being networked 'and all other entities who want to define their identities otherwise' (Callon, 1986, p. 208). These can be material barriers (prison walls), material organizations of space and time that restrict contact with outsiders (as in the physics program), discursive barriers (the imposition of incommensurable ways of categorizing or classifying the world), or barriers constituted through differences of taste, style and language.

As such interessements succeed in fixing identities and memberships, enrolment interrelates those roles and fashions the identities into systems of alliances. Interessement and enrolment are two sides of a coin: 'To describe enrolments is thus to describe the group of multilateral negotiations, trials of strength and tricks that accompany the interessements and enable them to succeed' (Callon, 1986, p. 211). Thus the physics and management programs weren't just setting up barriers to prevent their students from being 'captured' by other actor-networks, they were also weaving students into the actor-network by attaching them to each other and to particular material spaces and practices of representation. The end results were disciplinary constructions of the student. The question then is how these constructions were connected to the still-distant space-time orders of disciplinary practice.

Callon's answer is what he calls mobilization: the methods used to stabilize the enrolled coalitions in ways that 'ensure that supposed spokesmen for various relevant collectivities were properly able to represent those collectivities and not be betrayed by the latter' (Callon, 1986, p. 196). As Latour (1987) puts it, this means that it must be possible for whatever is being enrolled to be 'first displaced and then reassembled at a certain place at a particular time. This mobilization or concentration has a definite physical reality which is materialized through a series of displacements' (pp. 216–17). Techniques can range from mobilization in the flesh — assembling strikers for a mass rally, for example, or translating students into mobile practitioners of a discipline — to the representation of previously dispersed entities in stable, mobile, and combinable forms (textual or electronic).

I will use this concept of mobilization quite a bit, but with some qualifications. The Callon and Latour account of mobilization is preoccupied with the question of how actors at the center of a networking entity mobilize the people and things they are enrolling. It ignores the perspectives of those at the margins (Schwartz Cowan, 1987), and since much of what it means to be a student involves *being mobilized*, it is hard to formulate questions about education within the framework. Indeed, while Latour relentlessly treats scientific practice as a *construction*, he takes the practitioner, the scientist, as a given.

And there is an even more basic problem with an exclusively center-outward focus. From the center of an intersection things seem to come from every direction, everything is flow: from a distance, however, stable divisions and routes become visible. Adopting the *networker's* center-based perspective produces a neglect of issues such as class and gender domination, and the reproduction and maintenance of power structures (of which my focus, the *production* of disciplinary practitioners, is a part). One result, as Donna Haraway (1992) notes, is that in Latour's work enduring cleavages in the social order are ignored: '*any* consideration of matters like masculine supremacy or racism or imperialism or class structures are inadmissible' (p. 332). It would be a mistake to emphasize the fluidity of the world without noting that it flows at times in very deeply worn channels.[8] I will try to fit the 'actor-network' language, then, with a more general geographical conception of knowledge construction that allows for the existence of worn landscapes as well as flows.

To maintain this geographical interpretation and use it to look at disciplinary programs I'll make a distinction between 'material' and 'representational' productions of space-time.[9] This terminology is awkward — representations (books, pictures, etc.), after all, are always material (Williams, 1977) and material structures always have semiotic properties — but it distinguishes between constructions of space and time that are relatively immobile (e.g., a building) and those that are more mobile (a textbook or a body). Material productions of space-time, I will argue, played a key role in enrolling students into the disciplines, while representational productions of space-time were essential to the mobilization of practice and practitioners (although it was just the students who were being mobilized — both textually and physically — they themselves were also beginning to participate in practices of constituting and mobilizing the world distinctive to the particular disciplines). I will sketch out how I would like to use these terms in the next two sections.

Material Productions of Space-Time

No one should have difficulty with the idea that all activity has a spatial and temporal organization: that it's spread across specific physical regions and has a duration, a pace, a rhythm. What may be difficult is abandoning the 'physicalist' notion that space is merely a 'natural' container of activity, and instead accepting the idea that space is socially produced and contested. As Lefebvre (1991) puts it:

> (Social) space is a (social) product. . . . Space thus produced also serves as a tool of thought and of action; . . . in addition to being a means of production it is also a means of control, and hence of domination, of power; yet . . . as such, it escapes in part from those who would make use of it (p. 26).

The point isn't simply that portions of the environment are 'built', or that material spaces shape and constrain ongoing practice, it is that spaces and times themselves are produced and constituted through activity. Settings are always 'practiced', as de Certeau (1984, p. 98) puts it: appropriated, reworked, and given meaning by those acting in them and on them. People fashion and refashion the temporal and spatial boundaries that define an activity, who belongs with whom engaging in it, and where and when it can happen. Far from pre-ordained configurations of 'nature', settings and boundaries are products and objects of social struggle.[10]

Even if we insist on retaining a conception of 'natural' or strictly 'physical' space outside human agency, in the practical world such space is 'disappearing' (Lefebvre, 1991, p. 30):

> The initial basis or foundation of social space is nature — natural or physical space. Upon this basis are superimposed — in ways that transform, supplant or even threaten to destroy it — successive stratified and tangled networks which, though always material in form, nevertheless have an existence beyond their materiality: paths, roads, railways, telephone links, and so on. . . . Each network or sequence of links — and thus each space — serves exchanges and use in specific ways. Each is *produced* — and serves a purpose (pp. 402–403).[11]

Networks organize physical space as they produce and constitute the material spaces of social practice: buildings, offices, factories, and the channels of communication and transportation that move through and across settings. But 'practice' itself is not reducible to the observable activities of individuals in such local settings. Practice is distributed across the spaces and times it produces so that 'social interactions', 'settings', and 'events', are intersections of trajectories that tie together distant times and spaces and give them form as social space. Managers in their offices interact (literally, not metaphorically), with countless others they never see or become aware of as individuals. Physics students solving problems in groups late at night did not just interact with one another, but with their professors (who were safely in bed at home), their textbook authors (oblivious to the students' existence), and the practicing physicists scattered across the world whose works were reduced and simplified into the textbooks. This is the nature of 'interaction' in a world shaped by disciplines, networks and multi-national organizations; where 'face-to-face' interactions are no longer strictly local events:

> Once we start being concerned with the way encounters are carried on by their participating actors, it becomes clear that — even if it is plainly bracketed, temporally and spatially — no strip of interaction can be understood on its own . . . the forming and reforming of encounters necessarily occurs across broader tracts of space than that

involved in immediate contexts of face-to-face interaction (Giddens, 1985, p. 292).

Together, the networks that 'bind' (Giddens, 1981) large expanses of physical space-time and the practices of actors moving through networked settings create what Soja (1989) calls a 'socio-spatial dialectic'. This refers on the one hand to 'the physical and material flows, transfers, and interactions that occur in and across' those settings and embed them in networks stretching across space and time (Harvey, 1989, p. 218). On the other hand the settings themselves are the products of, i.e. they are constituted by, the movements of people and things. In Soja's (1989) words:

> Social life must be seen as both space-forming and space-contingent, a producer and a product of spatiality. The two-way relationship defines — or perhaps, redefines — a socio-spatial dialectic which is simultaneously part of a spatio-temporal dialectic, a tense and contradiction-filled interplay between the social production of geography and history (p. 129).[12]

Disciplinary power, in these terms, is about the production of space-contingent social life at the expense of space-forming social practice — about the stabilization of a disciplinary spatiality and the routinization of activity within that spatialization. As this implies, disciplinary practice assumes, as de Certeau (1984) puts it:

> a place that can be circumscribed as *proper* (*propre*) and thus serve as the basis for generating relations with an exterior distinct from it (competitors, adversaries, 'clienteles', 'targets', or 'objects' of research). . . . The 'proper' is a victory of space over time (p. xix).[13]

In later chapters we shall see how the physics and management programs create boundaries between the disciplines and the word. But if it's easy to conceptualize how disciplines use such boundaries to regulate the access of 'outsiders', it's much more difficult to see how people become 'insiders'. One of the major goals of the later chapters is to explicate the kinds of transformations required to spatialize and temporalize people in the form of disciplinary practitioners, to redistribute them as members of the disciplinary actor-network within disciplinary boundaries.

Here is a preview: as 'space-contingent' fields of practice, physics and management were unlike other programs (such as those in the 'liberal arts') in that they were localized in specific regions on campus — particular buildings, classrooms and corridors — and used organizational guidelines (e.g., course-taking requirements) to channel students, faculty and textbooks into those regions and exclude students from other programs.

In the physics program this localization of activity reached an extreme.

The program enclosed (physically) and compressed (socially) the spaces in which students worked, and monopolized their time. By their third year in the program most physics students were doing their work in small rooms with a small and relatively stable group of peers, and they were devoting the vast majority of their waking hours to physics work. The management program, by contrast, routed students into a bounded but much more inclusive material arena (a large 'business school' building they shared with other business majors in accounting, finance, etc.) in which many discrete settings (classrooms, cafeterias, study halls, interview rooms) were loosely connected. The activities of management majors were more diverse than those of physics majors (they spent less than half their time doing management work) and the students' time was fragmented into short unrelated units (both within a given course and across the longer durations of the term, the school year, and the degree program).

The other, 'space-forming', half of the dialectic was just as critical. Even within the greedy space-time organization of the physics program students did, and in a way *had to* appropriate the spaces and times of the programs and mold them to their own ends. Participation in small study groups, for example, was a creative response to the pressures of the program (though not the response of all students), that entailed the appropriation of classrooms and corridors late at night for student as opposed to departmental uses. On a different scale, management students regularly subverted the official pacing of their program by taking their courses in different groupings and at different times than the programs prescribed. Even in physics (where the number and sequence of courses was rigidly defined) students had some discretion over whether to take summer courses, how many courses to take each semester, and so forth.

The product of this dialectic was a trajectory through the material spaces of the programs that was, in both physics and management, linked to the formation of social networks among students and the creation of 'distributed' practices spread across groups of students and tools. It was along these trajectories that 'students taking physics and management courses' began to change into 'physics students' and 'management students'.

Representational Productions of Space-Time

Moving through the programs' material space-time, however, didn't make students into disciplinary practitioners. The physics and management programs were 'obligatory passage points' for people seeking their ways into the disciplines, but the disciplines didn't exist *in* the material spaces of the programs. Corporate 'management' was not enacted in the business school, and undergraduate physics students rarely did 'real physics'. Instead, I'll suggest that disciplinary practices were mobilized in representations — the contents of textbooks, lectures, and so forth — that flowed through the space-times of the programs along with the students.

It may seem odd to speak of distant spaces and times being 'mobilized' and collected at certain points, or of certain kinds of spaces being *created* in mobile representations, but consider: when we sit down and try to make sense of notes, transcripts, diagrams, pictures, memories, or any other kind of 'data', the settings where we took our notes and pictures and the interactions that produced our transcripts are no longer there, they have become distant from us in time and space. Phenomena are never temporally and spatially co-present with their representations; indeed, we do not know things as 'phenomena' until we inscribe them in some form that allows us to consider them at some spatio-temporal distance (cf. Haraway, 1988, p. 595). As Woolgar (1988) puts it, our representational practices constitute objects:

> The practical expression of, or reference to, a phenomenon both re-creates and establishes anew the existence of the phenomenon. In 'describing' a phenomenon, participants simultaneously render its out-there-ness. . . . The implications of isomorphism between textual organization and textual phenomenon are extremely important. Firstly, there is no sense in which we can claim that the phenomenon . . . has an existence independent of its means of expression. . . . Secondly, the notion of isomorphism suggests . . . not only that there is no object beyond discourse, but that the organization of discourse is the object. Facts and objects in the world are inescapably textual constructions (Woolgar, 1988, p. 73).

There is a similarity here to Foucault's (1972) notion of a 'discourse' — those 'practices that systematically form the objects of which they speak' (p. 49) — but what I'm interested in includes not just 'discourses' in this sense but also the less 'disciplined' improvisatory and informal representational practices of, in this case, students. In speaking of representations as producing space-time, I mean both that they functioned as 'signs and significations' of distant material spaces and practices (Harvey, 1989, p. 218), and that they were ways of creating or 'formulating' spaces without familiar physical analogs.

The idea of representations as signs or significations should not be problematic, but my concern here is not on what such representations *are* so much as what they *do*. They shape a space of practice by mobilizing — in the form of textbooks, cases, problems, equations, and so forth — physically distant disciplinary spaces (the 'real world' of physics and management practice, or to use Lave and Wenger's (1991) terms, the sites of 'full participation' in the field of practice) so that they can be transported into the educational spaces of the physics and management programs. As with any mobilization, of course, practice is subjected to a tremendous reduction: the educationally significant portion of what remains, what moves, is some portion of the representational technologies — mathematical equations, physical laws, ways of dressing, or ritualized forms of sociability — that practitioners use to produce and act upon the social space of the discipline. To *be* a physicist or manager means becoming proficient at the use of these representational technologies to the point of being able to move through and work upon spaces and times that are not accessible to people outside the disciplines: spaces and times that are constructions of disciplinary practice. Thus, educational programs preparing students for fields like physics and management — fields which consist in part of ways of organizing space and time through representations — connect themselves to those fields by incorporating mobile elements of them (equations, texts, machinery, etc.) into programmatic activity in central ways.

This binding of educational programs to disciplinary networks is just one manifestation of the disciplinary power constituted through representational organizations of space. If we think of 'power' as the ability to shape action across space and time (see Clegg, 1989 for distinctions among several conceptualizations of this ability), then systems of representation are core technologies of disciplinary power. 'How to act at a distance on unfamiliar events, places and people?' Latour (1987) asks, and answers:

> by *somehow* bringing home these events, places and people. How can this be achieved, since they are distant? By inventing means that (a) render them *mobile* so that they can be brought back; (b) keep them *stable* so that they can be moved back and forth without additional distortion, corruption or decay, and (c) are *combinable* so that whatever stuff they are made of, they can be cumulated, aggregated, or shuffled like a pack of cards (p. 223, original emphasis).[14]

When students took notes, worked problems, or analyzed cases, they were also mobilizing, moving and combining representations of disparate times and spaces. They couldn't 'be in' courses that were distributed across multiple spaces and fifteen weeks, but they could mobilize their course segments in notes, combine them, and in a sense hold the courses in their hands and review them as often as they liked, file them away and pull them out months later, or give them to friends.[15]

These practices were connected with those of disciplinary practitioners because in creating such mobilizations of their courses, students used representational tools — equations, ratios, case analyses, and so forth — similar to those used in disciplinary practice by physicists and managers to mobilize 'local' events, move them through space-time and combine them with other mobilizations. In this sense their academic practice reproduced the disciplines' social relations of power — what Dorothy Smith (1987, p. 3) calls the '*extralocal* mode of ruling' in which 'local actualities' are inscribed in 'abstract' (mobile, stable, and combinable) forms and transported to 'centers' such as laboratories, corporate offices, or university departments where they can be combined into sets of authoritative statements.

Educational practices, as components of disciplinary space-time networks, thus are not simply conditioned by relations of power, they are constitutive of them. In the programs I studied, students inserted themselves into power relations both by representing experience in the ways of the discipline (so as to become participants in the disciplinary accumulation cycle) and by representing themselves and their own experience in stable, mobile, and combinable forms (such as grades and transcripts), that allowed that experience to be transported to the disciplinary centers (the network nodes).

Reconstructing the Aims of Educational Studies

The 'geographical' view of knowledge and learning that I've sketched here represents a double break with the mainstream of educational studies. First, it departs from the psychological conception of the 'learner' as a discrete entity, an 'individual'. Instead it looks at actors as 'distributed', with shifting boundaries and compositions that spread across space as well as time:

> What is an actor? Any element which bends space around itself, makes other elements dependent upon itself and translates their will into a language of its own. An actor makes changes in the set of elements and concepts habitually used to describe the social and natural worlds. By stating what belongs to the past, and of what the future consists, by defining what comes before and what comes after, by building up balance sheets, by drawing up chronologies, it imposes its own space and time. It defines space and its organization, sizes and their measures, values and standards, the stakes and rules of the game — the very existence of the game itself. Or else it allows another, more powerful than itself, to lay them down (Callon and Latour, 1981, p. 286).

Students, all of us, are elements of distributed actors or actor-networks. When students enter college and begin to move along trajectories that reorganize them spatially and temporally as elements of actor-networks such as physics and management, the old divisions of 'learning', 'disciplinary reproduction', 'curriculum processes', 'identity construction' and so forth dissolve into knowledge in motion.

Narratives of a unitary or segmentable actor moving through time (upon which most of our notions of 'development' and learning depend) will no longer suffice. People stretch out in many directions at once and intertwine with other people and things distant from them. As Berger (1974) asserts:

> It is scarcely any longer possible to tell a straight story sequentially unfolding in time. And this is because we are too aware of what is continually traversing the storyline laterally. That is to say, instead of being aware of a point as an infinitely small part of a straight line, we are aware of it as an infinitely small part of an infinite number of lines, as the center of a star of lines. Such awareness is the result of our

constantly having to take into account the simultaneity and extension of events and possiblities (p. 40).

If we're no longer talking about cognitively and socially discrete actors, then we can get rid of the decontextualized 'problems' and 'tasks' of cognitive psychology. If people are spatially as well as temporally distributed, then students in classrooms (and people generally) aren't simply interacting with the other people and objects physically present in the settings. They are also interacting with all of the distant spaces and times that they carry with them and that went into the constitution of those actors and objects. A 'task' or 'course', to borrow Rosaldo's (1989) characterization of ritual, is:

> a busy intersection . . . a place where a number of distinct social pro-
> cesses intersect. The crossroads provide a space for distinct traject-
> ories to traverse, rather than containing them in complete encapsulated
> form (p. 17).

Each element of a setting such as a college class, textbooks as well as people, are 'mobilizations' of other spaces and times moving along trajectories intersecting in the settings of the programs. Instead of specific tasks, problems, or courses, the unit of analysis is the system or network of such elements defined by the recurrent patterns of intersections of the various space-time trajectories. Unique or rare intersections, although common in everyday life, are of less interest for understanding constructions of knowledge, which presume organizations of space and time that bend trajectories across each other on multiple occasions.

This suggests a second break that follows from the first. If people are spatially and temporally distributed and courses are the fluid intersections of elements stretching out across and moving through space and time, then the problematic we have to make sense of is the network of relations that tie things together in space and time: to understand what's going on in one intersection we have to look at the mesh that connects it to other intersections. The logic or sense of an event or a setting can never be found entirely *within* that setting and event. As Smith (1987) puts it:

> The everyday world is neither transparent nor obvious. Fundamental
> to its organization for us in this form of society is that its inner
> determinations are not discoverable within it. The everyday world, the
> world where people are located as they live, located bodily and in
> that organization of their known world as one that begins from their
> own location in it, is generated in its varieties by an organization of
> social relations that originate 'elsewhere'. . . . The everyday world is
> not fully understandable within its own scope. It is organized by
> social relations not fully apparent in it nor contained in it (pp. 91–92;
> cf. Giddens, 1985, p. 292).

These breaks detach us from the traditional questions of studies of education and learning. Instead of focusing on the social forms of knowledge and their acquisition, we're inquiring about the structure of networks, the ties that bind them, and the nature of whatever it is that flows through them. In the chapters that follow, then, my concerns are not the *disciplines* of physics or management (see, e.g., Traweek, 1988; Jackall, 1989; Whitely, 1984), nor am I studying physics and management *students*. Instead, I'm dealing with the structure and articulation of the curricular networks in undergraduate physics and management, and students' trajectories through them.

Notes

1 'Trajectories' has been variously used by social theorists (Anselm Strauss, Anthony Giddens, and others) to describe patterns of change or development. Although I use the term, I share de Certeau's (1984) reservations:

> 'Trajectory' suggests a movement, but it also involves a plane projection, a flattening out. It is a transcription. A graph (which the eye can master) is substituted for an operation; a line which can be reversed (i.e., read in both directions) does duty for an irreversible temporal series, a tracing for acts (pp. xviii–xix).

De Certeau's remedy — a special use of the very common terms 'strategy' and 'tactics' — seems awkward too. However, the sense in which I use trajectory is close to de Certeau's notion of 'strategy':

> a calculus of force-relationships which becomes possible when a subject of will and power [what I'll call later 'actor-networks'] . . . can be isolated from an 'environment' [i.e., can differentiate spaces and bind them together into center-periphery/inside-outside relationships]. A strategy assumes a place that can be circumscribed as *proper* (*propre*) and thus serve as the basis for generating relations with an exterior distinct from it (p. xix).

2 British and Scandanavian researchers didn't take such a reductive or dismissive stance towards social context and produced studies of how college students interpret and address tasks depending on the work contexts in which the tasks are embedded, and how different study strategies are associated with different fields and the tasks typical of those fields (Entwistle and Ramsden, 1982; Saljo, 1981; Marton and Svensson, 1979; Pask, 1976; Ramsden and Entwistle, 1981). Even this work, however, remains preoccupied with discrete individuals and ignores classroom processes and the social organization of study and learning. I have cited this work from the 1970s and early 1980s because it represents some of the most thoughtful research that has been done on study in college. In more recent work, however, some of these researchers cited have begun to move towards the Vygotskian perspective discussed below (e.g., Marton, 1984; Saljo and Wyndhamn, 1990).

3 In his critique of some critics of cognitivism (Suchman, 1987; Coulter, 1983); Woolgar (1987) points to the 'danger of merely substituting a social for a cognitive mechanism' (p. 325) for explaining behaviour. As Latour (1990) puts it, 'Great divides',

such as the one between the mind and society, 'do not provide any explanation, but on the contrary are the things to be explained' (p. 20). Although they occasionally see through these issues, some Vygotskians seem to become preoccupied with questions of 'internalization' and the relationship between 'inter-' and 'intra-psychological' processes (e.g., Newman, Griffin and Cole, 1989), without seeing that the inter/intra distinction itself is problematic and that internalization is an issue only if one takes a static view of space and time as background conditions through which autonomous individuals march. Lave (1988) and Lave and Wenger (1991) do attempt to dissolve the divide, but as I will explain later, I find elements of their work problematic.

4 Vygotskians are not unaware of these issues, but they address them only in passing, and then in a vague and inadequate fashion (see, for example, the final chapters in Lave, 1988, and Wertsch, 1985), or they attempt to reduce structural issues to face-to-face encounters (see, for example, Engestrom's discussion of the Manhattan project (1987, pp. 267–78). White and Siegal (1984) come close to attacking this problem directly, but end up embracing a modified version of ideas from ecological psychology. If anything, issues of spatiality and temporality, and the linkages of political economy to situated activity that those issues highlight, are receding further from view. In her more recent work, for example, Lave (Lave and Wenger, 1991), who at least acknowledged these issues in her earlier work (Lave, 1988), is now focusing on despatialized 'communities of practice' which she and Wenger treat as discrete and autonomous.

5 The use of the pronoun is tricky. As Haraway (1991) comments 'You or I (whatever problematic address these pronouns have) might be an individual for some purposes, but not for others' (p. 216).

6 Compare these ideas to Bateson's (1972) discussion of 'mind' as the distributed unit of evolution. Bateson asks: 'Suppose I am a blind man, and I use a stick. I go tap, tap, tap. Where do *I* start?' He argues:

> the way to delineate the system is to draw the limiting line in such a way that you do not cut any of these pathways in ways which leave things inexplicable. If what you are trying to explain is a given piece of behaviour, such as the locomotion of the blind man, then, for this purpose, you will need the street, the stick, the man; the street, the stick, and so on, round and round.
>
> But when the blind man sits down to eat his lunch, his stick and its messages will no longer be relevant — if it is his eating that you want to understand (p. 459).

As I read this, Bateson is saying that the distribution of mind is a construct shaped by the analyst's explanatory agenda. My argument is that distributed network organization is *constitutive* of knowledge and practice. Bateson's argument works because he treats the blind man as an object and ignores the social relationships in which the blind man participates (cf. Smith, 1987): how are walking down the street and eating lunch socially organized? How do such activities fit into the blind man's ongoing practice? My aim in this book is not to explicate discrete events but to look at students' ongoing practice as they move towards participation in disciplinary networks, and to understand how that practice is organized in and organizes space-time relations.

7 Again note the contrast with Lave and Wenger's (1991) idea of 'communities of practice' as loci of learning (I contrast my position with this one not because I find it weak, but on the contrary because it is compelling). For them 'knowledge' is *within* the community; in the actor-network framework knowledge is a power-laden construction of actions upon an exteriorized world.

8 Clegg (1989), I think, is responding to this problem on some level when he re-
works the actor-network concept in terms of what he calls (following DiMaggio
and Powell, 1983) 'organizational fields'.

> Such fields exist only to the extent that they are an achievement of epis-
> odic power in the institutional field, stabilizing relations of power between
> organization agencies A, B, . . . N. Episodic power's achievement will con-
> sist, first, in constituting a relational field by 'enrolling' other organiza-
> tions and agencies; second, in the 'stabilizing' of a network of power
> centrality, alliance and coalition among agencies within the field; third, in
> the 'fixing' of common relations of meaning and membership among the
> agencies within that field, such that they are reflexively aware of their
> constitution as a field (p. 225).

This may well be a better language for talking about physics and management as
disciplines, but it doesn't seem flexible enough to allow me to talk about the
production of physicists and managers. Thus I retain Callon's terminology.

9 This distinction is inspired by Harvey's (1989), and bears some similarity to Castells'
(1991) 'spaces of place' and 'spaces of flow'. All of these distinctions are indebted
to Lefebvre's work (1991). However, what I mean by 'representational organization of space-time' is different than what Lefebvre (1991) calls 'spaces of representation' or 'representational spaces'. The former is:

> conceptualized space, the space of scientists, planners, urbanists, techno-
> cratic subdividers and social engineers . . . all of whom identify what is
> lived and what is perceived with what is conceived (p. 38).

The latter is:

> Space as directly *lived* through its associated images and symbols, and
> hence the space of 'inhabitants' and 'users', but also of some artists and
> perhaps of those, such as a few writers and philosophers, who *describe*
> and aspire to do no more than *describe*. . . . This is the dominated — and
> hence passively experienced — space which the imagination seeks to
> change and appropriate. It overlays physical space, making symbolic use
> of its objects (p. 39).

I am not altogether sure that this distinction can be sustained — in physics for
example, representations of space and representational spaces (space 'perceived'
as opposed to 'imagined' in Harvey's terms) seem to dovetail — but insofar as it
can be my work here is probably concerned more with representations of space
than representational spaces. In any event, my main interest is in how 'representational organizations of space-time' are used to 'mobilize' the world and organize
actors across space and time.

10 Willis's (1981) study shows that in arenas of education such as compulsory schooling, the material organization of space-time is an object of struggle. The 'lads' he
describes are contesting the material organization of space-time promulgated by
the school, and performatively constituting in its place the space-time relations of
working-class life. They don't organize a competing network of 'representational
spaces', however, and thus continue to be incorporated into the school's representational networks — grades, examination scores, certificates, etc. Advancing themselves within the strictly local network, the 'lads' have few resources for overcoming
the friction of distance that separates them from the spaces of social power. They
are subjugated within the larger space-time networks linked by representations.

11 Lefebvre (1991) should not be taken as suggesting here that there is some pristine 'empty' space that has to be socialized through human practice:

> The notion of a space which is at first empty, but is later filled by a social life and modified by it, also depends on [a] hypothetical initial 'purity', identified as 'nature' and as a sort of ground zero of human reality. Empty space in the sense of a mental or social void which facilitates the socialization of a not-yet-social realm is actually merely a *representation of space*. . . . Of an actual historically generated space, however, it would be more accurate to say that it played a socializing role (by means of a multiplicity of networks) than that it was itself socialized (pp. 190–1).

12 Lave's (1988) distinction between 'arenas' — durably organized settings not directly negotiable by the individual — and 'settings' — the individual's personally 'edited' version of the arena (pp. 150–1) — could have some bearing here (although the distinction is too static and reminiscent of the cognitive psychologist's 'task environment' 'problem space' distinction). Unfortunately, Lave (1988) gives a physicalist slant to her comments on 'arenas' (following Barker's ecological psychology) and in practice ignores them, refusing to trace out the connections between grocery shopping and production networks, marketing systems, family-work structure and the myriad other connecting networks. Lave and Wenger (1991) drop the whole matter altogether and make few connections to Lave (1988) — apparently seeing no use for the conceptual apparatus developed to describe grocery shopping in their discussion of learning in apprenticeships.

13 Lefebvre (1991) articulates a similar but more generalized view of the modern state as a spatializing entity:

> The state is consolidating on a world scale. It weighs down on society (on all societies) in full force; it plans and organizes society 'rationally' with the help of knowledge and technology, imposing analogous, if not homologous, measures irrespective of political ideology, historical background, or the class origins of those in power. The state crushes time by reducing differences to repetitions or circularities (dubbed 'equilibrium', 'feedback', 'self-regulation', and so on). Space in its Hegelian form comes back into its own. This modern state promotes and imposes itself as the stable center — definitively — of (national) societies and spaces (p. 23).

Like de Certeau, Lefebvre is careful to emphasize resistances to this state of affairs — 'state-imposed normality makes permanent transgression inevitable' (p. 23). My point is merely that disciplinary power and state power share a similar spatial underpinning.

14 De Certeau (1984) makes a very similar argument:

> . . . the scientific method requires a delimitation and simplification of its objects . . . there corresponds to the constitution of a scientific space, as the precondition of any analysis, the necessity of being able to *transfer* the objects of study into it. Only what can be transported can be treated. What cannot be uprooted remains by definition outside the field of research. Hence the privilege that these studies accord to *discourses*, the data that can most easily be grasped, recorded, transported, and examined in secure places. . . . Of the practices themselves, science will retain only movable elements . . . or descriptive schemas . . . leaving aside the aspects of a society that cannot be so uprooted and transferred to another space (p. 20).

De Certeau and Latour, of course, are looking at this process from opposite perspectives: Latour from inside the laboratory (the only exception being Part II of Latour, 1988), de Certeau from outside.

15 'Stability', 'mobility', and 'combinability' are of course defined in terms of an actor-network: they are accomplishments, not essences within entities. It takes an elaborate system to constitute textual forms as stable, mobile and combinable (as in physics) — and it doesn't always work (as in the management program).

In this connection, the emphasis here on writing and printed text requires some comment. As a number of commentators have pointed out (Marcus, 1991, pp. 401–2) systems of electronic communication have introduced radical changes into the organization of communication and work in fields such as physics, and the printed text has declined in importance as a technology for organizing the discipline across space and time. Some, like Poster (1990), make radical claims for the reorganizations of space and time that follow from the new technologies: Poster suggests that electronic communication networks have no space/time coordinates: 'electronic language . . . is everywhere and nowhere, always and never. It is truly material/immaterial' (p. 85). One would think that computer hook-ups materially organized across space and time will continue to be necessary, but in any event I merely claim that in *undergraduate educational practice* — at least in the mid-1980s at the university where I was working — writing and print retained dominance. Even in the very few cases where computer programs were used (e.g., the simulation games in business programs) they functioned as analogs of printed text. That is, they lacked channel-distinctive properties or effects.

Chapter 2

Producing Material Space-Time and Constructing Students in Physics

My interest in spatial issues grew partly out of my fieldwork. The fellowship that funded this study didn't allow the university to take overhead money, so I was forced to make do without an office, a mailbox, or a storage locker. To do the fieldwork I had to borrow university spaces to write, read, and conduct interviews in during the day. I could read and write in a lot of places, but when I made interview appointments with students we had to arrange to meet somewhere on the campus — I asked the students to suggest places — and then find a place to talk.

After a while it dawned on me that when students suggested possible meeting places for the interviews I was getting a glimpse of what the urban planner Kevin Lynch (1960) would call their 'environmental images' of the campus — a list of the places where they spent time, worked, studied, or just places they considered significant public landmarks. With most students, it seemed, these images were idiosyncratic. My meetings with management, education, and sociology students were scattered all over the place: many in the student union, others in bars, cafeterias, at the library, at the tennis courts, in hallways, stairwells, lounges, and even some outdoors. My meetings with physics students, however, were always in one place: the physics building, an architecturally austere, 15-story structure set apart from the rest of the campus.

I thought this building an unwelcoming place. During the daytime it had no quiet corners or unclaimed spaces for sitting, talking or writing. There were no spaces for students to congregate in or appropriate for their own uses. Aside from classrooms on the first two floors and a small, eerily quiet library that always seemed to be crowded with desperate freshmen cramming for tests, the majority of building space — essentially all of the upper floors controlled by the physics department — was taken up by faculty offices and laboratories.

These were professional workspaces which students avoided and where, in fact, they seemed unwelcome. Most students told stories of abusive treatment when they went to professors for help, and by their third year few even bothered to try. In any event, it wasn't all that easy to *find* professors. Few put their names on doors or indicated office hours. The directory on the ground floor was quite inaccurate. If you did catch a faculty member in his office, you had to wait to see them in halls empty of chairs or benches, leaning on the wall or sitting on the floor.

And yet, this building was the center of the academic and social universe for students majoring in physics. It dominated their environmental image of the campus. Third- and fourth-year physics students spent almost all their time there. It was where they socialized and worked, and where they wanted to meet me, even though we always had trouble finding a place to talk.

This paradoxical role of the building in the students' lives — the way it marginalized them while they treated it as their center — makes more sense if we think of the building as a material space·moving in time. Consider the one area in the building ceded to undergraduate activity: a corner of a corridor near the departmental offices where there were three large tables with folding chairs, and next to them movable chalk boards. During the day these tables belonged to engineering students in the introductory physics and engineering courses who came for help with their homework. Late at night, however, they became the property of the physics majors. As Arnold, a senior, explained, the tables were 'surrounded by non-majors looking for help [from graduate assistants] during the day'. But 'at midnight or two o'clock in the morning' the tables were taken over by juniors and seniors. Several fourth-year physics students, like Alice, said this corner was where they spent their nights: 'on the third floor, where all those physics help tables are. There are quite a few people who study there.' Other students talked of appropriating the then-empty classrooms as night-time workspaces.

While management students could manipulate or negotiate program requirements to make them fit in with other interests, the physics program seemed successfully to suppress its students' non-physics interests (or to make students pay for them by extending their stay in college and lowering their grades). When I interviewed Alice in an upper hallway of the physics building she talked about her love of literature and other things unrelated to physics:

> My biggest literature interest is in modern poetry, modern American poetry. Eliot and Frost, Corso and Ginsburg, all the Beat poets. . . . I read *Vogue* in my spare time, too, I like to sew my own clothes so I like to copy patterns out of there. . . . I listen to jazz, I listen to folk music. I play the clarinet, and have really stopped playing with any group right now, but I have just always had a real fondness for music.

But she almost never did those things. Alice spent, by her estimate, 'eighteen hours a day', in the physics building, going to class, doing homework problems, studying. When I asked her if that was an exaggeration she answered:

> When I'm not sick and behind I spend — I have classes here all morning, I have classes all morning somewhere, and I spend the afternoons here. And sometimes at night I study here.

Although Alice's eighteen hours may have been extreme, all of the physics students seemed to be putting in deadly hours at the physics building, and for some like Arnold there was no escape even when they left: 'I live with a lot of physics majors, so at home is going to be a group studying around the table situation as well.'

Along with this spatial localization of students there was a particular patterning of time and a narrowing of student interests. To see how the program accomplished these things I am going to look at how the material organization of space-time produced by the program funnelled students into a small physical zone — those few floors of the physics building — and into the temporal regime that claimed the vast majority of their waking hours. What I'll try to describe in this chapter is how this 'compression' of space-time (Harvey, 1989) separated physics majors from other students and melded them into study groups (consisting of people, texts, and tools) that worked homework problems and prepared for tests. To belong to one of these groups meant in essence becoming enrolled in an actor-network that connected students to the disciplinary network of physics. In the next chapter I will look at how the representational organization of space-time in the program — representations of space on paper and representational spaces produced in texts — strengthened this (albeit still loose) connection of students' activity to the social space of physics practice itself.

Standardizing Space

In prestigious physics departments it's the graduate programs that receive most attention; they compete with other physics programs for prestige — the graduate program of the department I studied was ranked in the top twenty nationally in terms of faculty reputation, (Jones, Lindzey and Coggeshall, 1982) — and, according to the department head, the graduate programs have prior claim on the 'better' professors. By contrast, undergraduate programs like the one I studied were seen mainly as places to prepare students for graduate school (which is not to say that all of the students actually ended up there).

In spite of their secondary status, undergraduate programs play a key role in physics education. Nationally, graduate programs in physics depend almost exclusively on undergraduate physics programs for their students and serve as the major 'market' for such students (see AIP, 1988b; Porter and Czujko, 1986, p. 72). This dependence has led to a kind of colonization of undergraduate physics, a pressure to standardize the undergraduate curriculum so that students entering graduate schools can be assumed to possess the same level of training regardless of the undergraduate program in which they studied. This pressure, coupled with the growing national dominance of a relatively small group of graduate physics departments in the post-World War II period,[1] had by the 1960s produced a national standard for the number and type of courses considered appropriate in undergraduate programs (Physics Survey Committee, 1972, p. 761):

> The minimal four-year undergraduate program of instruction for a physics major at the four institutions surveyed [Berkeley, MIT, Columbia, Swarthmore] contains an average of forty-three semester-hours of physics, nineteen semester-hours of mathematics, and nine semester-hours of chemistry. (Nationally, the undergraduate preparation for graduate work in physics requires around thirty-six-hours of physics and eighteen semester-hours of mathematics.) (International Union of Pure and Applied Physics, 1966, p. 77)

The physics department I studied had modelled its course-taking requirements after this national pattern — in 1986 undergraduate majors were required to take a minimum of forty hours in physics, twenty-four in math, and eight in chemistry — to make its graduates interchangeable with graduates of other respected undergraduate programs across the nation. The sequence in which the courses could be taken also became standardized. By the early 1970s it began with:

> an introductory course covering the full range of physics, now always including calculus and extending over a period of one to two years. . . . The dominant curricular progression in the junior and senior years embodies a more or less canonical sequence of courses that deal in greater depth with special areas of physics. Thus, most of the topics are repeated, but this time with the use of differential equations, computer programs, and some reference to current research. Such a sequence of courses typically includes classical mechanics, electricity and magnetism, optics, thermal physics, electronics, and quantum physics (Physics Survey Committee, 1972, pp. 762, 763).

I found this basic pattern in the program I studied some fifteen years later — the major differences being that electronics had become an optional course and a full four courses were devoted to various aspects of quantum mechanics (see Appendix 1).[2]

This national standardization of program structure played a key role in disciplinary reproduction by making it possible to overcome the geographical separation of undergraduate programs and link them together tightly, merging them in a sense, in textual space. From the perspective of the discipline this linkage homogenized and stabilized the supply of personnel destined for graduate programs (where people begin to engage in the 'real work' of physics), and made it possible for programs scattered across the country to communicate quickly.

It follows, however, that with such a tight standardization of curriculum, the 'problematization' or definition of allowable identities and interests that the program constructed for undergraduate physics students was very narrow, and there were enormous pressures to exclude students who could not adopt the appropriate identities. As I said earlier, students were expected to go on to graduate school in the field, and from there to careers as professional physicists. If that wasn't what they had in mind, one professor explained, 'they're making a mistake [majoring in physics]. They should be in engineering.' All of the students I interviewed said similar things.

The undergraduate program can be understood, then, not as a site for the infusion of physics knowledge into students' heads, but as a path (itself composed of many intersections) shaping a lock-step trajectory through a curriculum that restricted students' activities to a small set of material spaces dominated by the discipline. The end product was a highly restrictive social space that tied together practices spread across great physical distances.

Weeding Out Students

This space-compressing trajectory began even before students entered college. High school physics and calculus courses were necessary prerequisites for pursuing physics in college: the vast majority of undergraduate physics majors nationally were drawn from these courses, and 90 per cent of entering graduate physics students had passed through them (Porter and Czujko, 1986, p. 71). This tight linkage was an historical construction. Post-Sputnik concerns over the quality of science education had allowed faculty to boost the 'sophistication' of their undergraduate courses, which in turn demanded the creation of a highly selective system for funnelling the 'brightest' students into the field. As one professor explained, in the early 1960s:

> There wasn't enough modern physics [in the undergraduate curriculum], it was almost entirely classical physics in those days. And people thought that with such bright students at the undergraduate level we ought to be giving them graduate material. . . . This was a national movement. We introduced [the Introductory Mechanics] . . . designed for physics majors, which required at least one semester of calculus.

Increasing the complexity and difficulty of the undergraduate curriculum meant restructuring high school math and science curricula so that, in effect, they became downward extensions of the university curriculum (Pallrand and Lindenfeld, 1985, p. 46). Since the introductory university physics courses required calculus preparation and presumed at least some familiarity with physics concepts, high school courses in these areas became the critical gateways into the spaces of the discipline.

Students' chances of taking such courses were determined largely by where they went to high school. Students at suburban schools with predominantly white student populations were more likely to have taken such courses than students from schools with large poor or minority student populations (AIP, 1988a). When physics courses *were* available at the poorer schools they were generally of inferior quality (Sweet, 1988, p. 94).

Even by high school, then, the spaces of physics education were highly restricted and, not incidentally, gendered. Only 19 per cent of high school seniors took physics in the early 1980s — 26 per cent of the boys and 14 per cent of the girls; and only 8 per cent took the calculus required of beginning physics majors — 10 per cent of the boys, 6 per cent of the girls (Raizen and Jones, 1985, p. 98).[3] The results are programs, like the one I studied, where 90 per cent of the students were male, the vast majority from middle or upper-middle class suburban schools, and almost all white.

Moving from high school to the university just intensified these space- and socially-compressing forces. First-year physics students began their academic careers in classrooms and dormitories shared with students in other programs, but by their third year their academic activities were localized in the physics building. Along the way the range of their social contacts at the university narrowed and their time was organized into tight schedules dominated by physics work. This compression of space-time was set in motion by organizational mechanisms designed to winnow the number of students majoring in the field.

The lower division course sequence — introductory mechanics, introductory electromagnetism, and waves — was, in the words of one professor, 'designed to weed out students. It's used by the college. I would say of the people that register, about 25 per cent fail.' Courses designed to flunk large numbers of students are not uncommon in higher education, of course, though their function varies across disciplines. Hacker (1989), for example, points to the practice in engineering programs of simply suppressing the supply of graduates. She quotes one professor as saying to his students that '90 per cent of you would make good engineers, but only 40 to 50 per cent will graduate' (p. 42). The attitudes of faculty in the physics program I studied were less cynical: instead of restricting production they thought of themselves as simply dismissing the students who lacked the skills and commitment to study physics. Physics professors boasted about the high failure rate and said it was a 'natural' feature of physics programs:

> Generally in any physics course about 30 per cent of the class will fail, unless it's an upper division course for physics majors where there's already been some weeding out. But if the course is taught at the same level consistently, 30 per cent of the class will flunk. I don't know why that is. It's independent of the teacher, it's independent of the textbook, it's independent of anything. We've discussed it a lot among ourselves. It seems that you just keep building the complexity of the material and you eventually reach a point where everybody but the people who really can become physicists give up. And it seems to be independent of how far you go. A guy can be a physics major and take five physics courses and then all of a sudden he flunks. . . . We grade rather leniently otherwise everyone would flunk. So if somebody who makes a C or B might be making less than 50 per cent of

their work. And so it's not surprising that sooner or later he reaches a point where he flunks.

The 'leniency' in grading, as the professor put it, meant 'curving' the grade: defining the mean score as a 'C' or 'B' and awarding grades above and below that in terms of their distance in standard deviations from the mean. Of course, this produces a distribution in which about 30 per cent of students *must* flunk out. As students recognized, grades and learning were not closely connected:

All physics grading is done on a, you know, normalized type system, where the average grade is usually a high C or a low B. . . . The average grade on one test I took was a 32. . . . One person was in the 40s, one was in the 50s, one was in the 60s and one was in the 70s. Probably two-thirds of the grades were in the 20s. . . . And so the professor comes along and normalizes and says, okay, everybody who made up to 20 gets a C, 20 to 35 gets a B, and everyone above that gets an A. And so maybe that's an indication that the test was too tough, or that the professor's not teaching the material well, or that none of us give a crap — something like that — but still it just ends up that the grades are given on how well the class does. . . . It's very possible that no one could be learning anything and yet you still get people with As and Bs and Cs and Ds . . . (Luke).

The 'weeding out' accomplished by such grading practices meant that only a minority of the students who began the program as freshmen made it to the third year. As one professor put it:

The freshmen and sophomore classes always fill up; but by the time you get to the first junior class we're fighting for ten students. . . . we're just on the verge of not having enough undergraduates to teach upper division undergraduate courses (Marker).

The social space of the program imploded. Students who survived began to describe the selectivity of the program with a pride that quotations like this one can't quite convey:

The physics undergraduate department is small, I don't know how many students we graduate each year, thirty, something like that, at the most? It's not a big number, ever, I mean, it decays exponentially, the number of people in physics, it really goes down, especially the first two years (Alice).

As Traweek (1988) suggests, the students who survived this winnowing began to see themselves as part of 'an extremely restricted community' (p. 78) of elite students in elite institutions. At the same time, however, their sub-ordinate status in that community was forcefully communicated to them. The physics program had a boot-camp mentality, an equation of learning with suffering. Even 'successful' students occasionally felt overwhelmed by the work and could get 'bad' grades. If we ignore the vast majority who got weeded out and look at all the students who successfully *completed* degree programs in physics over a one year period, 29 per cent actually *failed* at least one physics course, and many others had 'withdrawn' from physics courses, presumably for academic reasons. None of the management graduates whose transcripts I examined, by contrast, had failed a management class.[4]

Temporal and Spatial Boundaries

The physics programs began to monopolize student time from the freshman year onward. In the very first physics course students were typically required to do large, weekly 'problem sets'. In theory the homework was supposed to supplement other forms of study. As one professor warned in his syllabus for introductory mechanics:

> You are kidding yourself if you don't put in about three hours of study time for every hour spent in class, not counting time spent on home-work. Study with the aim of understanding, memorization is worthless.

Students, however, described homework problems in the introductory courses as so time-consuming that they had little time for other kinds of study. Lem, for example, recalled that:

> One of the things you get out of your early classes is you get used to doing a lot of homework. That may sound kind of funny, and it is, but it's true. I mean, when I was in high school I whipped through home-work in five minutes towards the end of class and I never had home-work in high school because I'd do it right then. . . . So when I got here I wasn't used to like spending most of the night doing problems and getting three or four hours sleep. And the massive quantities of homework they tend to give you in initial classes teaches you that you're going to have to do that [stay up all night working], if not through difficulty then just through sheer volume.

It should be understood that the homework problems were just one of the work-intensive requirements students faced: they boasted of crushing work loads. Once, for example, as I prepared to leave a study group session around midnight (it had begun about 9.30 p.m. and was still going strong with six students present), Glen mentioned that he hadn't slept the night before be-cause he'd been studying for a test. Laurie responded with a litany of her own study requirements: after her physics lab earlier in the day she'd spent two hours studying rocks for a geology test before coming to this study session, and on top of that she had a German test coming up which she wouldn't be able to study for at all, not to mention the study that *would* be required for a vector calculus test later this day.

The inelasticity of time created by this kind of schedule and by the tight pacing of work within physics courses, meant that falling behind almost always led to failure:

> Last semester, for my first quantum test, I studied for approximately two weeks. That's about eight hours a day. That's fourteen days at eight hours a day, and I still made a middle D on that. The bottom line is that you just have to stay very on top. And as soon as you lose that on-top feeling and position, you're really sunk. Because it's almost impossible to regain an on-top position once you're behind (Paul).

For the students who survived these trials-by-time in the introductory courses and remained in the program, physics became an even more time-greedy, enveloping major.[5] By their third year, almost all student coursework was in physics and math, in required courses strictly sequenced by prerequisites. This concentration of coursework, and the problem-heavy nature of those courses, created 'interessements' in the form of temporal streams or boundaries that separated physics students from other actor-networks into which they might be enrolled (e.g., fraternities, sororities, etc.). When other networks did prevail, as in the case of two students I interviewed, enrolment in physics was forestalled. One of those students, Melvin, spent most of his time outside class with relatives who lived in the area:

> I don't have really very many close university friends. I have nephews and nieces who are near my age, and I have two sisters here. My parents are here right now. And most of my socializing, I guess, is done with them.

Without friends among the other physics students Melvin worked alone, failed several physics courses, and ultimately abandoned his plans for graduate school. In the case of the other student, Luke, it wasn't relatives but a fraternity he'd joined prior to his freshman year that monopolized his time. He did all right in the introductory physics courses which covered material familiar from high school, but quickly encountered problems with the upper division coursework:

> Second semester was the first physics class, and I did real well in that — but I'm sure that's because I'd had two years of it in high school. And the same kind of thing happened with my sophomore year, taking the other two lower division physics classes. I didn't do as well, just

because the stuff we'd had in high school wasn't quite up to the same level, but still I spent almost no time doing it, I spent a lot of time at the fraternity. And so my grades started to go down, and by the time second semester sophomore year hit they were pretty low, and I'd managed to destroy a pretty good GPA. And then first semester junior year was rock bottom. That was the end of it. And I kind of got an ultimatum from home and that type of thing. . . . I just did not have the study skills that it takes, the daily grind type of thing. I had no idea what it took to do that. And I would try to do the homework the night before, by myself, and I would just get frustrated because I couldn't do the first one, so I'd blow it off. Then I'd have no idea what was happening on the test.

After failing some upper-division physics courses he switched his major to secondary school science education.

Unlike the management students I'll describe later, who cultivated local ties outside the university to gain practical experience and develop contacts with potential employers, physics students did better if they avoided local ties (even to the department: there was an expectation they'd go elsewhere for graduate school). Their enrolment in physics, then, was the product of a struggle among actor-networks (programs, families, fraternities) in which material organizations of space-time, in particular temporal and spatial boundaries, played a critical role in organizing bodies. Bob, for example, compared physics to his other courses, and explained that the latter were:

a lot easier. So that changes your whole attitude towards it . . . if you put more than five hours into it, or even if you put that much time into it . . . that's the most you could ever think of putting into it. And in a lot of the physics classes I took, you would be putting in problem-solving and studying and reading — but mainly in problem-solving, you'd be putting in anywhere from, ah, nine to twenty hours a week. There was one semester where we counted up the hours that we had been working out of class, in physics, and it was, it averaged out to over twenty hours a week. Most of it was problem-solving. And with the other classes that you take, unless you're in a math class, . . . there's not really any problem-solving. And the only thing that you really have to keep up with is reading. And you might have to write an occasional paper, but . . . that wasn't difficult. They're mainly just comparing things.

Alice gave a breakdown of how that kind of time was spent:

Oh, [you spend the greatest amount of time on] the physics, by far. You spend for each physics class probably seven, eight hours on a homework assignment each week. And that's over and above studying for tests. It doesn't include any of that kind of work or going over chapters or rewriting notes. It takes me a long time to do a physics homework assignment. . . . Working problems either for homework or for just practice, to learn the material.

Required physics and math courses accounted for over half the physics students' total undergraduate coursework and almost all of their upper-division coursework. The courses colonized the students' time outside of class and focused it in a specific material setting. Students spoke not just of spending all their time on physics but, as we saw at the outset of the chapter, of spending it in a relatively small set of locales. The curriculum stabilized students' identities as 'physicists' by creating space-time barriers that cut them off from alternative networks. The result was a distinctive socio-academic mechanism of 'enrolment' in physics — a way of stabilizing identities as physics students through alliances: the study groups.

Study Groups

When I began my fieldwork my notion of problem-solving in physics was shaped by the classic cognitive science studies of 'expert' and 'novice' problem-solving in physics (see Nespor, 1990a). These studies describe problem-solving as something that happens in the head, or at most in an encounter between the head and a pencil and paper. For some reason, probably because I'd gone through college working mostly by myself, I easily accepted the idea of study and learning as an individual encounter with 'subject matter'. Then the first physics student I interviewed, Arnold, disabused me of this idea by explaining that most of the students in the program studied collaboratively in groups. I gradually abandoned my collection of 'think aloud' protocols of problem-solving and instead began to talk to students about the groups and to sit in on group meetings when I could.

Although I saw one professor encourage students to work together, the study groups I saw were student initiated and organized. The groups emerged in different ways. Liz, a sophomore just beginning to work in groups, ex-plained the genesis of her group this way:

There's a group of us that are friends. We had Intro. Chemistry to-gether, some of us were in mechanics together, some of us were in E&M together. And it happens that we all have this class together, so we get together. Some of the people there are added — I guess you could consider them part of the core group now, because they're in other classes we're in now. So they know we're studying and they come along and study.
Nespor: Ah, did you have study groups like that in mechanics and E&M, or did you do problems with other people?

Not in mechanics. Mechanics we weren't — well, a lot of those people weren't in my mechanics class, and the ones that were, we weren't that close yet, to get together and study. Some of them did separately, but I didn't with them. Ah, in E&M, we — had some study groups, mostly before tests though, not every week to do the homework. This is the first time we've really had a set time and place that everyone goes to every week to do the homework.

Regardless of the path, by their third year in the program most physics students had settled into a routine of collaborative work. As Liz's comments suggest, most of this work focused on homework problems, and for several reasons, the problems can been seen as a major determinant of the study-group format.

First, instruction throughout the physics curriculum revolved around sets of homework problems, assigned weekly, that led to mid-terms and final tests. This problem work gave a cyclical, weekly rhythm to students' activity. Second, the large number of required courses students took together, the sequencing of these courses by prerequisites, and the 'weeding out' practices described earlier, meant that by the beginning of the third year (the Classical Dynamics and Modern Physics courses) classes were small (about twenty students) and students were interacting with the same classmates from class to class: 'I mean, you could say we form a new group for every class, but there's the same people in every class' (Alice) 'It's virtually the same [group of students] class every time' (Karl).

Finally, once the population had been compressed this way any competitiveness that might have been produced by the strong exclusionary pressures in the early courses was replaced by a logic of cooperation. Students talked of working together as a necessity for survival in the program, and the evidence, in terms of the kinds of grades they made, supports that claim. Glen, for example, said that while he:

> could probably do the homework by myself, I don't think I would get as good a grade, and I don't think I'd get as much out of it. Because I get other people's viewpoints. I may look at a problem and try to figure it out with a way that's real real difficult. And I may get the answer. But somebody else may say, 'look, this is a lot easier method to do it, or this is a lot easier way to look at it.' And it really helps. And also you can help other people with your knowledge. And not only does that help them, it helps you. If you can explain it, and learn how to explain it to somebody else, it just so much reinforces your own knowledge. And I really think that that's a good way to do it. Get with a bunch of people (Glen).

The physics students I interviewed considered their textbooks opaque, their lectures 'boring' glosses on the book, and, with a few exceptions, their faculty aloof. Several, when I asked them about going to professors for help, told me an anecdote about asking professors for help with a problem and being told something like; 'I did this twenty years ago, I don't need to do the homework' (Melvin) or (and Paul's referring to a different professor than Melvin):

> I went to him one time and I said, 'well, I'm having a hard time with this problem.' He looked at me and said, 'well, I solved it twenty years ago, now it's your turn.' What a jerk (Paul).

For us these comments are nice illustrations of the stability and standardization of the curriculum across time and space. For the students they were emblematic of the way the program placed interpretive responsibility on their shoulders. In this context, study groups were a way for students to construct a supportive environment. As Arnold explained:

> We all depend on each other from class to class. These tables up here on the fifth floor, although they are surrounded by non-majors looking for help during the day. If you come up here at midnight or two o'clock in the morning and there's a group of us trying to do these problems. A couple of different years represented, the older years helping the younger years. There's a lot of that.

Working in groups helped students discipline themselves to the long hours required in the program: Arnold spoke of how he and his group partners 'forced each other to study'. But the group work sessions were also social occasions that made the work bearable and occasionally fun: full of joking, jockeying for status, and conversations that sometimes digressed far from the academic tasks. By the students' own accounts, the many hours they spent together in and out of classes and in the study groups created close friendships among group members and locked them into friendship networks that excluded non-physics students (the women, for reasons I explore shortly, were exceptions, having friends unconnected to physics in addition to a core of physics friends).

Bob's account illustrates the trajectory of students' involvement in the groups. He transferred into the program from another university in his second year and at first had been socially unconnected. He explained:

> Basically what I'd do, if I knew anyone in the class, then, I'd just ask them if they wanted to get together and study sometime on this stuff. And we mainly worked on homework and we reviewed some for the tests, but ah, if I didn't know anyone specifically, then I would just kind of take pot luck, and maybe the people who were sitting around me, or someone who seemed like they asked a lot of questions in class and knew what was going on, I'd see if they wanted to study.

Ultimately Bob became part of a stable study group, and the members of the group became his close friends:

> Since there's a core set of courses, you usually go through them at the same time. There turned out to be some courses that you weren't taking with your other friends, depending on how they arranged their schedules it was sometimes different, but usually there was at least one person in your class that you had been in a class with before. . . . I studied for maybe a year to two years with just the same people . . . you get to be real comfortable around them and you get to know them very well. And we've all become pretty good friends.

These comments suggest that working in groups was in part a conscious strategy for doing well in *physics* (the students didn't study in groups for their other courses).

> To me, I think either you're extremely bright or you're a fool if you don't get in a study group. Because you save so much time, simply because when you sit there, even if you're trying to explain a problem that you already understand to someone, you learn it that much better by explaining it. And you find out what you don't know while you're trying to explain it. Also, if you're having a problem with something, then someone else might have a different viewpoint on it so they might understand it a little better. And there's also the fact that you're not sitting by yourself for five and six hours on end, pounding over a problem — instead you sit in groups of four or five and pound over them for four and five hours (Bob).

Taken as a whole, the spatial and temporal organization of the undergraduate program enrolled students in a physics network by compressing the material spaces in which their activity unfolded, monopolizing their time, and distributing their activity across other students — and as I'll suggest in the next chapter, across material instruments (pencil and paper, chalkboards) and artifacts (textbooks). When the physics curriculum succeeded, then, it tied its students very tightly to the physics network — but it didn't always succeed.

Partial and Failed Enrolments

There were clear incentives to participating in study groups. Of the students I interviewed, those who worked in groups had grade point averages of 3.0 or above (on a 4.0 scale), while those who worked individually, that is, whose spatial and temporal relations included people, places and times outside physics, had grade point averages below 3.0. The 3.0 level is significant because it's usually the minimum required for admission to a graduate physics program (although it's by no means the only selection criterion — Graduate Record Examination [GRE] scores and letters of recommendation also count).

All of the students I talked to were aware in a general way of the academic advantages of working in a group, but some none the less refused to participate, and not everyone who did participate 'belonged' to the groups in the same way.

Women were marginalized in study group activities.[6] If the groups were distributed actors, their gender was male. All of the women I interviewed belonged to study groups. All of the study groups I observed had women in them. However, the very group processes that assisted academic performance pushed women toward peripheral positions in the groups. The pressures weren't overt. None of the women I talked to felt 'discriminated' against, and Alice even speculated that 'if anything, people remember me because I'm a girl, and so it's an advantage for that reason.' But the nine to one male/female ratio seemed to produced a pernicious dynamic. Male students monopolized the discussion and women's comments and questions were ignored or not treated as serious (see Nespor, 1990a).[7] Thus while women were enrolled in the physics network and took on identities as 'physics students', they were relegated to a kind of 'knowledge-weak' identity (Nespor, 1990a). Sometimes this became fairly obvious in the interactions. This exchange, for example, comes from one sophomore problem group:

Liz: Could you do this without putting an m in there, just by putting a K in there?

Mick: [To Liz, after thinking a moment] [Laughs]. What, just putting a spring in there? . . . You could, but that would be an entirely different problem and that's not what they asked for [general laughter].

Liz: Okay, come on [embarassed].

Mick: In fact, if you want to, what you could possibly do is, well, let's see, if you have K over m. . . .

Liz: Well they also say springs and masses . . .

Mick: Yes, I know — okay, well, if you want to put another spring under here you'll have 4 degrees of freedom and two masses and it really gets nasty.

Liz: So you'll just solve that for K over m.

Hours later in the same session I heard Liz exclaim: 'I finally got one before somebody told me how to do it.' I can't claim this kind of deflation of self-confidence was shared by all the women in the program, but it was widespread. Even Alice, a senior cruising through the curriculum with a 3.9 grade point average, told me:

I don't have quite as natural an ability as I think a lot of other people do. Some women, but more men. There's just more men in physics. It's an incredibly, overwhelming majority.

Most of the women in the program were either uncertain about continuing in the field or had decided not to. Debbie, a senior, wanted to get into the astronaut program rather than continue in physics. Liz, a sophomore in the middle of the weedout courses, felt 'under a lot of pressure' and was thinking of switching majors out of physics even though it was her main interest. And when Kelly, a classmate of Liz's, said she didn't want to go into academia her explanation was 'I look at my physics professors and I say: "Do I want to be like this?" No.' Any interest she would have in physics, she explained, would be in teaching it: 'I would only do it [become a professional physicist] if I felt like I had a real talent for being able to get things across to people.' Similarly, Alice, who did want to continue in physics, said the thing she looked forward to most in graduate school was being able to teach. None of the male students mentioned teaching as something they wanted to do.

Part of the reason for this disenchantment with the discipline was that the space-compressing and time-greedy nature of the curriculum stringently limited the time the women could spend with female friends or male friends who weren't physics students (as best I could tell, the women in the program did not band together or work together). Just being *in* the field could compromise one's social life outside it, as Kelly explained: 'Some people are shocked: "You're a physics major?" and then the conversation kind of lags.' Even when the women could work a 'second shift' to build a social life, the long-term trajectory of a physics career put tremendous stresses on it. Alice, for example, described her situation thus:

> I'm dating someone now, but I don't expect anyone to follow me off to wherever I go to grad school. Wisconsin is a possibility — I mean, I don't even know if I want to live there for that many years. It's just not considered the thing for a man to follow a girl somewhere, wherever she decides to go. It's usually the other way around. And I just couldn't see settling down until I get out of grad school, I just think it would be real hard. It's sort of weird because a lot of my friends are beginning to think, you know, friends who are engaged — are thinking it's sort of odd because I don't have any thoughts of that. Sorry, I have at least six more years of school.

Alice's plight was the consequence not of simple discrimination but of the way physics as a discipline produces a highly restricted and compressed social space in order to stabilize activity across vast distances of physical space. The undergraduate program moved students towards the discipline by compressing their spatial practices, but the trade-off for being able to move fast and far within the network was not being able to move in and out of it very easily. The network itself, however, stretched across many universities: as tight and hermetic as the program space seemed it was open to students from physics programs at other institutions, and it explicitly prepared students for other programs. This kind of network required actors who could move across the distances it organized with relative ease not only textually (as we'll see in the next chapter) but bodily. Women's bodies, as Alice's comments suggest, were culturally constructed as less mobile than males, or rather, their mobility was seen as dependent upon the mobility of males.

The women in the program, then, were only 'partially enrolled' in the physics actor-network. Overwhelmed numerically in the program, marginalized in the study groups, socially isolated, women might succeed in finishing the program with good grades, but seemingly at the price of their identification with the field.

Some men in the program were only partially enrolled as well, but for different reasons than the women. Instead of being marginalized in the study groups they declined to participate in them and developed other enrolments into the physics actor-network. Their social backgrounds played key roles in shaping these strategies of participation.

Most of the students in the program (at least, I should say, most of the students who'd survived to be seniors) came from quite affluent backgrounds: both Arnold and Eric had fathers who were executives at major computer corporations, Luke's father owned his own software company, Alice's father was a supervisor for a state government commission, and so on. There were two students who came from 'working class' backgrounds: Paul, whose mother did 'clerical work' (his father had died when he was in junior high), and Lem, whose father was a truckdriver. Unlike the other students I interviewed, both *commented*, unsolicited, on their parents' occupations. Paul, for example, called his mother's work 'excruciatingly mainstream' and explained his interest in the experimental side of physics in terms of his repugnance for the kind of paper-focused work she did:

> I think that's part of my repulsion to that. It's sterile. Non-inspiring, non-stimulating in an intellectual way. I get a lot of feedback in what I do, what I do with my physical self. I get a lot of feedback in the way I feel emotionally and intellectually also. And when I find things out of the ordinary that require thinking about things in an unordinary way, then that's stimulating all the way around. It keeps me interested and thinking, I like that (Paul).

Lem tried to explain the discontinuity between his trajectory though schools and his parents', providing an elaborate explanation of how his father and mother could be 'intelligent' even though they didn't have high status jobs:

> My dad is a truckdriver, which in my opinion is a real shame, because he's an intensely bright individual. He has no problem figuring things out. I'm not saying I'm bright. I'm not that conceited. I don't know, maybe I am, maybe I'm not. I just have a gift for figuring things out, and he has that same gift. I know he's intelligent. He's just lazy. In high school he used to get Ds and Cs because he never did his

homework — not because he did badly on the tests, he did well on the tests, he just never did the homework . . . it was boring. He'd rather go out and play with his friends or whatever. And he wasn't interested in going to college. He doesn't like school and I can't blame him. My mother is also a very intelligent woman. And she's much more intelligent than she allows people to think. I don't know why. It's not like my father discourages that. He's always yelling at her, 'oh come on, don't ask me, just do it', but for some reason she seems to tend to — I don't know, in a crisis she will stand up and just do what she wants, but a lot of the time she will defer to other people for some reason. I don't understand why. I'm not like that at all (Lem).

What makes these kinds of comments interesting is the way they contrast with the other physics students' answers when I asked them what their parents did: flat descriptions without commentary. But if Paul and Lem felt estranged from their families in some way, they had not 'acculturated' to the physics program, nor did they seem to want to.

Both, although they were aware of the benefits of group work, eschewed participation in study groups. Elsewhere I've discussed their decisions in terms of Bourdieu's (1986) notions of cultural capital, arguing that their tastes, interests and styles of interaction made them uncomfortable working with the upper-middle class males who dominated the groups (Nespor, 1990a). Here I want to highlight how the spatial practices of the students attached them to the physics network in different ways than their peers.

Paul had done poorly in high school and ended up going to a 'state technical institute' (a kind of trade school) where he trained to be an electronics technician. Finding work as a technician unsatisfying he decided to get a university degree in physics (though the university refused to give him credit for his technical institute courses and forced him to begin in the freshmen courses). His low grade average notwithstanding, Paul's technical skills quickly got him a job that moved him into the spaces of physics practice earlier than his peers. Unlike most of the other undergraduates, who linked themselves to physics through textual practices (in classrooms and problem-solving sessions), Paul won a niche as a device-maker in an experimentalist's lab:

I'm much ahead of my contemporaries, just by the fact that I've got a two-year degree and can design electronics. In physics there's not a lot of coursework designed to familiarize people with electronics. There's one course in the undergraduate curriculum, maybe two, but they're mickey mouse, by and large. . . . And so I can design things, and that's helped me out immensely.

Paul avoided the other students in his classes and explicitly rejected the study group format for doing problems. He worked alone at home or in his office space at the lab:

I don't enjoy interacting with the undergraduates in physics because they have a very unsophisticated view of physics. They haven't ever done it. And I can be as snobbish as I like, so to hell with them. . . . So when it comes to solving problems, I don't talk to people. If I can't get a problem I consider that a personal failure, and I will just work harder on the problem.

Paul made poor grades in part, as he saw it, because he approached life differently than other physics undergraduates:

I try to experiment and get things that are really outside of the physics train of thought, just because you can become, and this happens time and time again, people are so completely monomaniacal that they're just geeky idiots that know nothing about anything but how to solve the Schroedinger equation or something like that. And they're not able to carry on a conversation to people that are outside of their field. And I think that's really a shame. They're just not well-rounded.

Some of the other male students in the program were sensitive to this kind of criticism. Arnold, for example, made it a point to tell me that 'a lot of us are quite involved with intramural sports, do a lot of that' (though still 'with other physicists'). But the mainstream male students like Arnold were, at least in my interviews with them, very insular, speaking from the perspective of the program. Paul and Lem, on the other hand, were openly critical of aspects of the program, and our conversations ranged much more widely over non-physics issues.

Alone among the undergraduates I interviewed, Paul had his own space in a lab (space usually reserved for graduate students, post-doctorates, and professors) and associated mainly with graduate students. His experience working in major laboratories left him feeling that the temporal organization of undergraduate life was simply unrealistic:

[In the undergraduate program] your time frames are divided up: 'Okay, I've got a semester and I've got weeks and I've got classes and if I do do it I can do good or bad.' And everything is very compartmentalized and your time frame is — everything is done for you. You can lead your life mindlessly. And you can sit and think and eat and sleep, and that's all you really have to do. Every single time frame, time dimension, is figured out for you. And the real world of doing science is completely different from that. You have to set up your time frames completely for yourself and if you do it poorly, if your time frames are a little too long, then you get called on the carpet by your superiors.

The other working-class student, Lem, used terms similar to Paul's to describe other physics students:

Most of my friends are not physics students. . . . [Most physics students] are very introverted and like all they think about is physics, all they want to think about is physics, apparently. You can't strike a conversation up with them about much else. They seem to be quiet and just basically boring. . . . They sit in libraries with books and read and that's boring to me. There's a whole world out there and you've got to try and experience it, in my opinion, to be a well-rounded person.

Lem didn't work in complete isolation, however: almost alone among the students I interviewed he spoke of regularly consulting with professors (not necessarily those from whom he was currently taking courses) about his work, of having found several with whom he could talk about problems.

Both Paul and Lem, then, had found niches in what was usually 'faculty' space. While this may have given them more 'mature' or 'well-rounded' orientations to physics in some sense, it left them terminally marginalized, with no routes to fuller participation in those spaces. By doing their coursework independently of other students, Paul and Lem were never enrolled in the 'distributed actors' that populated both the graduate and professional levels in physics. Learning to work as the member of a team was more than a strategy for academic success, it was an accomplishment that began to shape students' capacities for participating in the dominant forms of social relations in the professional work of the field.[8] Paul was, at first glance, an exception, but the niche he had carved for himself in the laboratories was a strictly subordinate one. Instead of collaborating on the design of experiments he made devices for them to others' specifications. He worked *for* teams rather than as a member of them.

It was striking, in fact, that in addition to Paul and Lem, all of the women I interviewed except Debbie (who wanted to be in the astronaut program) preferred the *experimental* side of physics to 'theory', and that these were the only students among those I interviewed who had decided on the experimentalist route. Beasley and Jones (1986, p. 38) argue that this 'predilection for theory' is common among entering graduate students in physics, something they attribute to a lack of 'meaningful laboratory experience' at the undergraduate level. This is a plausible explanation (the laboratory component of the program I studied was weak compared to those of similarly ranked programs, and the most prominent faculty members were theorists), but it is also true that the students who chose the non-theoretical emphasis were also the ones marginalized and self-excluded from the work groups, suggesting that the groups fostered or at least supported the 'theoretical' orientation towards physics. It was this orientation that Alice, even though she participated in the study groups and made very good grades, seemed to feel herself unequipped to pursue:

I don't have the mind to want to sit and do abstract reasoning. Which is what theoretical physics is to me. I mean I can't see the connections as well between the ideas. I'd rather do 'how does the theory apply to the real world?' I don't really want to sit and derive new theories. I want to test them. I want to see what they do.[9]

I return to the issue of how group work shaped students' practice of physics in the next chapter and suggest there that the study group was a social space supporting particular representational productions of space-time: productions of disciplinary spaces on and in paper in mathematized, 'abstract' forms. In brief, as students moved through the physics curriculum representations of reality became more and more detached from the spatiality of everyday practice and hence it became more and more important for there to be a cohesive network — like the people, textbooks, and problems that made up the study groups — to maintain and enforce the representational practices that produced the space.

The 'learning' that took place wasn't a matter of internalizing knowledge — as Luke pointed out in his explanation of grade normalization earlier, passing and failing weren't necessarily connected to knowing anything — but neither was it a matter, as Lave and Wenger (1991) would argue, of performing authentic physics at the periphery of a community of practitioners. They suggest, for example, that:

> ... There are vast differences between the ways high school physics students participate in and give meaning to their activity and the way professional physicists do. The actual reproducing community of practice, within which schoolchildren learn about physics, is not the community of physicists but the community of schooled adults [is this a 'community' in the same sense as physicists constitute a community?]. Children are introduced into the latter community (and its humble relation with the former community) during their school years. The reproduction cycles of the physicists' community start much later, possibly only in graduate school (pp. 99–100).

But this line of argument works only if we accept an atemporal and despatialized conception of 'community'. The fact that high schools and undergraduate colleges are institutionally separate from graduate or professional physics doesn't mean the realms are unconnected: they are, in fundamentally important ways. As I showed earlier, where you attend high school is crucial to your chances of becoming a physicist. The fact that undergraduate students (or high school students) aren't doing 'real' physics doesn't mean that what they're doing isn't an essential part of the trajectory to doing 'real' physics. Nor is it the case that high school and undergraduate programs are simply allocative mechanisms sorting students: they were also, crucially, moving students into configurations, distributed actors, that could move within and work upon the space-time of the discipline.

This distribution of students in actor-networks is a necessary part of the process by which the discipline assures the use and intelligibility of its key representational organizations of space-time. We can give a kind of answer now to the question Latour (1988) asks:

> What is this society in which a written, printed, mathematical form has greater credence, in case of doubt, than anything else: common sense, the senses other than vision, political authority, tradition, and even Scriptures? (p. 51).

It is, in the case of the physics program, a narrow society of people bound together by tight social ties and spatial practices that compress the world into small material spaces strongly bounded off from other social networks. And now we can turn to the second quandary Latour provides:

> Most of the 'domain' of cognitive psychology and epistemology does not exist but is related to this strange anthropological puzzle: a training (often in schools) to manipulate written inscriptions, to array them in cascades, and to believe the last one on the series more than any evidence to the contrary (Latour, 1988, pp. 51–2).

In the next chapter I will examine how this training was accomplished in undergraduate physics.

Notes

1 By the early 1960s, twenty-five institutions received almost 60 per cent of all federal funding for physics (Kevles, 1977, pp. 396–7).
2 There is variation nationally in the number and type of laboratory courses offered by undergraduate physics programs, and in the amount of emphasis placed on quantum as opposed to classical physics (Physics Survey Committee, 1972, pp. 763–6). As undergraduate programs at similar insititutions go, the one I studied had relatively light laboratory requirements.
3 Among the physics students I interviewed all but two had taken physics and calculus in affluent high schools. Attendance at such schools also increased students' access to university-produced physics curricula such as PSSC and Project Physics. Access to such programs strongly influenced the likelihood of students entering and continuing in physics as a career. Thus while only about 9 per cent of US high schools offered the PSSC program and only about 8 per cent the Project Physics curriculum, students with access to these programs were over-represented among those who eventually received Bachelors in physics. About 25 per cent of the undergraduates who earned Bachelor's degrees in 1983–84 had taken PSSC in high school, 12 per cent had taken Project Physics (Pallrand and Lindenfeld, 1985, p. 47).
4 The percentage is based on an examination of the transcripts of all physics graduates at the university over a one-year period. At least one professor justified the high failure rates in the introductory courses by an appeal to history:

When I was an undergraduate in physics our first real course, this was back in 1958, this was the first upper division course for physics majors, the first that really used a lot of calculus, I remember 50 people in it. . . . It was a two-quarter course. The second quarter there were five. [The attrition rate] is university-independent, teacher independent, course independent, as long as the course was of the level of sophistication that the normal physics course is.

5 The consuming character of work in such fields is seemingly independent of one's interest or commitment to the discipline. Hacker (1989), who was studying engineering programs, reports how she found herself neglecting her other responsibilities and devoting all her available time to study. This experience is reminiscent of Burawoy's (1979) experience of 'making out' on the industrial shopfloor, of being captured by the game of work almost against one's will.

6 The progressive gender segregation of physics began in secondary school and intensified over the years:

Although one-third of all high-school graduates who have taken physics are women, only 14 per cent of the physics Bachelor's degrees are awarded to women. . . . Women represent a small percentage of physics graduate students and . . . fewer than 8 per cent of the new doctorates were earned by them (Porter and Czujko, 1986, p. 76).

The processes I describe at work in undergraduate education may be quite different from those in K-12 public school or in graduate school.

7 Although some commentators on women in science education (Head, 1985; Smail, 1987) draw on Gilligan (1982) and Lever (1976) to suggest that women are disadvantaged in competitive group activities because of values or developmental factors, I would emphasize instead their token status in the groups as the key factor in the construction of their identities as 'knowledge-weak' (cf. Kanter, 1978). For research casting doubt on the generalizability of Lever's arguments, see Goodwin (1988) and Eder (1990).

8 Memory, Arnold, Stewart and Fornes (1985) analyzed authorship patterns in nine fields (modern languages, philosophy, political science, business, discipline psychology, botany, education, chemistry and physics) and found collaborative efforts to be much more common in physics than the other fields. This appears to represent a trend over time. By 1981 the average number of authors for papers in *Physical Review Letters* was 4.87. (Memory *et al.*, 1985, p. 270). In 1971 it had been only 2.25, a relatively small rise over the average of 1.75 in 1936 (Brooks, 1978, p. 105). To some extent, the rise in collaborative work reflects changing emphases in the types of physics being done. For example, the 1981 average number of authors of papers in the areas of fluids and plasmas was only 3.23; in elementary particles it was 11.2 (and for experimental papers in elementary particles it was 28.03) (Memory *et al.*, 1985, p. 271). As Memory and his colleagues argue, 'The cost of doing experimental research in physics is probably the chief reason for this collaboration. Economy of scale compels researchers to share scientific equipment' (p. 270).

Kleppner (1985) notes that small-scale group research — a few graduate students working with a professor or researcher — is still the dominant form of training for physics graduate students (he estimates it characterizes the training of about 70 per cent of graduate students in physics) (Kleppner, 1985, p. 85).

9 Readers familiar with Sally Hacker's (1989;1990) work on learning to be an engineer will have noted some similarities and contrasts to her accounts. This might be a good place to mention them. The physics program I studied was not as competitive as Hacker's engineering, nor were students working on 'problems with clear and

singular answers', working 'toward the test and not understanding' (1989, pp. 41, 42). I never saw any of the joking (1990, pp. 118–20) that Hacker describes. In contrast to the fetishism and eroticization of technology in engineering, physics students prized 'theoretical' skills (again, this could be a function of the particular culture of this program). The similarities, however, are just as strking: the greedy nature of the curricula, the 'inelasticity of time' as Hacker puts it, and the mathematization of the field created a 'daily experience [that] required control of sensuality, the emotions, passion, one's very physical rhythms' (1989, p. 56).

Chapter 3

Connecting Students to Practice: Mobilization in Physics

Scientists start seeing something once they stop looking at nature and look exclusively and obsessively at prints and flat inscriptions (Latour, 1986a, p. 16).

The total amount that a physicist knows is very little. He has only to remember the rules to get him from one place to another and he is all right . . . (Feynman, 1965, p. 45).

Physics was a struggle for me. I collected textbooks during the fieldwork but I couldn't 'read' them as I read other books (nor, as it turned out, could the students). I could 'follow' the lectures in the lower division classes but I'd forget quickly and I never knew how to start the problems even when the math and concepts they required were well within my grasp. Students let me come to their study group sessions, and occasionally they'd stop to repeat something for me, but a lot of steps in the definitions and solutions of problems went unstated — they involved conversions and transformations that students took for granted — and a lot of the 'discourse' took place through quickly scribbled, then revised or erased diagrams and equations that I couldn't copy down (my audiotapes of these sessions were usually useless and I didn't have the resources to videotape).

I had to keep reminding myself that I wasn't trying to 'understand' physics or management the way the students did. To do that I'd have had to enrol in the actor-networks of the disciplines myself (not just take or observe the courses, but become a physics major) — and what I was trying to do instead was understand how the students *got connected* to those actor-networks. Instead of trying to interpret or analyze texts — books, problems, or whatever — my interest is in how texts and their uses produced spaces and times and spatio-temporal relations. Undergraduate physics education was scattered across a set of heterogeneous locales — departments, programs, courses, classrooms, laboratories. To organize these spaces into the kind of 'network' that could connect students to flows of disciplinary practice, activities in one space had to be transformed into representations that could be sent across space without changing much. They had to be mobilized.

A Chain of Mobilizations

Physics consists in part of discipline-specific representational technologies for constructing phenomena and spaces and times that are not accessible in our everyday material spatial practice. In professional practice machines play a critical role in these processes (Traweek, 1988), but at the undergraduate level of education most of this work is still done through writing. Writing produces its own spaces. Textual practices can mobilize the disparate, widely-scattered phenomena of everyday material practice and bring them into a work setting and under the control of practitioners. Textual practices can also create spaces and times outside everyday practice — the space of dreams, poetry, cosmology, quantum mechanics. In physics education these two uses come together. The everyday world is mobilized and then reconstructed in an esoteric form.

Instead of talking about students 'learning' physics, then, I'll talk about the pathways and trajectories that entangled them in the discipline's representational productions of space-time. Although this entanglement didn't make students practicing physicists in any sense, it did crucially connect them to the discipline. The media of this connection were the textbooks, notetaking, and problem-solving practices that involved the students in the use of equations and mathematized representations and mobilizations of the world. This process wasn't something that happened all at once. Instead, students gradually moved into physics across the years of their academic careers.

The representational organization of space-time in the physics program was built through a recursive network of courses. Students covered topics in 'mechanics' and 'electricity and magnetism' three times: in the two lower division introductory courses, in the upper-division 'classical dynamics' and 'classical electrodynamics' courses, and then, as Alice put it, 'when you get to be a graduate [student] you do it again. Three times.'[1] Instead of seeming repetitive, students and faculty said that the second and third passes through the topics treated them at 'deeper' levels. In one professor's words:

> Students can get a superficial understanding of the topics in their freshman year, but they're not really able to apply these concepts; in fact they're not even aware how superficial their understanding was until they face more difficult problems later on. I find that most of the students in the class seem to feel that they're encountering the topics for the first time, even though they had the basic concepts in their first year or their second year. . . . In fact, in my own experience as a student I recall I didn't really feel comfortable with classical mechanics even after receiving my PhD and I was horrified to learn that my first teaching assignment was classical mechanics at the introductory and intermediate levels. It wasn't until I had several years of teaching experience at those levels that I found myself comfortable with mechanics.

With each encounter topics were constituted in increasingly mathematized forms that squeezed the world into a diamond of numbers. When students and faculty talked of a deep as opposed to 'superficial' understanding they meant a *mathematical* understanding. One of the students, Bob, gave this analysis:

> Like with [introductory] electricity and magnetism we'd just have a basic algebraic equation; and with the class I had in classical electrodynamics we . . . started off with a stationary electron, and derived everything in static electric theory. And then we made the electron move, and then we derived all of the rest of electrodynamics from a single moving electron. And you learn so much more. I mean, you *derive* all the algebraic equations. And it was a lot more complex, and it was a lot more difficult. But it was also a lot more interesting. [. . .] It was mainly you look at everything at a deeper level. And instead of, say, looking at *how* is it — oh well, it's done this way — you look more at *why* is it — and it's done this way *because* of these things. And the same goes for the classical dynamics. That was also a very interesting course. . . . I don't think we covered a whole lot of different phenomena [from the lower-division courses], but we mainly just looked at them at different levels. We looked at, ah, LaGrangians and Hamiltonians, all of these in classical dynamics. And you start looking more at the energy in the system, where you looked before more at just, well, we looked at, well, the pendulum would swing this way — and it just swings that way — and we'll say, well, we know the pendulum swings that way, why does it swing that way?

In physics, diagrams and mathematical equations — among the most stable and movable of representations — formed the bedrock of a representational technology that was shared (but employed in very different ways) by professional physicists and beginning students (cf. Latour, 1987, pp. 240–1). When the professor spoke of being 'able to apply concepts' he was talking about being able to deploy such representations.

To move representations like equations across the different kinds of spaces that make up a disciplinary network, however, they had to be mobilized in different kinds of containers for different kinds of journeys. The different mobilizations were like links in a chain connecting students in the program to the practices of physics long before they actually entered that field of practice. In the program I studied there were four critical links in this 'chain of mobilization':

(1) The equations of physics were mobilized in textbooks that linked physics practice to physics education, and connected geographically dispersed educational programs.

(2) Within the program, professors mobilized the equations in the textbooks in their lectures, transforming them into linearly produced chalkboard representations.

(3)   Students mobilized these equations in the lectures in their class notes, to be scrutinized and recombined in study and problem-solving activities.

(4)   The problems in the textbooks mobilized the equations, linking together types of problems and shaping how students moved through the representational space-time.

The product of these mobilizations was a progressive stripping away of the 'everyday world' and its replacement with a mathematized world. To see how this was accomplished I shall examine each mobilization in turn.

Textbooks as Educational Mobilizations of the Discipline

If, as Harvey (1989) suggests, 'the written word abstracts properties from the flux of experience and fixes them in spatial forms' (p. 206), then we can see physics textbooks as spatial forms that mobilize distant physics practices (albeit in a specially reduced form) and make them available in classrooms. Textbooks can serve as mobilizations in part because they are constructed in a distinctive rhetorical style: they are made up of statements that lack 'modalities'. References to agency (e.g., the author), the agent's actions, and the antecedent conditions of those actions are excluded from the text (Woolgar, 1988; Latour and Woolgar, 1986, pp. 75–81; cf. Olson, 1980). Why? Because such modalities would link the statements in the books to ongoing practices: every modality makes a statement more mutable, less mobile, less easily combined with other statements. When modalities are excluded, as in textbooks, a statement takes on the character of a context-independent universal that can be moved across space and time. It is rendered:

> devoid of any trace of ownership, construction, time and place. It could have been known for centuries or handed down by God Himself together with the Ten Commandments. It is, as we say, a fact (Latour, 1987, p. 23).

By making statements stable and movable in this fashion, it's possible to use them to facilitate communications across distances and tie together networks of practice spread out in space and time. At the same time, the denser and more tightly organized such networks, the more easily they can create and maintain facts. As we saw in the last chapter, physics is a tightly woven network of institutions dominated by a relatively small number of highly funded departments and labs that can define what counts as 'physics' and what counts as an adequately prepared graduate.

This standardization of curriculum is accomplished through the use of textbooks that are highly standardized and demodalized in form and content.[2] In this sense, textbooks define the undergraduate physics curriculum. They demarcate discrete subject areas and levels, and define the basic topics to be addressed at each level.[3] Thus most of the graduate programs described in the handbook of *Graduate Programs in Physics, Astronomy, and Related Fields* (AIP, 1985) define expected levels of undergraduate preparation in terms of five or six textbooks. For example:

> *Undergraduate preparation assumed*: For graduate work in physics it is assumed that the student has an undergraduate background that includes the following: mechanics at the level of Symon, *Mechanics*; electricity and magnetism at the level of Cook, *The Theory of the Electromagnetic Field*; thermodynamics at the level of Rief, *Fundamentals of Statistical and Thermal Physics*; atomic physics at the level of Morrison, Estle and Lane, *Quantum States of Atoms, Molecules, and Solids*; quantum mechanics at the level of Park, *Introduction to Quantum Theory* (AIP, 1985).

The particular books listed vary from program to program,[4] but the books at each 'level' are generally similar. Once set, the configuration of books used in a particular program is difficult to change because of the tight prerequisite linkages between the required courses: a substantive text change at one level would disrupt the entire sequence. As a result, there is a very slow turnover in textbooks:[5]

> [The undergraduate students] all will take courses later on for which this is a prerequisite, and consequently the subject matter has been decided upon by essentially a department course and curriculum committee. And it will not stray very much from that. Students must cover a certain number of topics. There's a textbook committee made up of people who have taught the course — four or five people — and they will go over various textbooks and select the one that most closely tracks the subject matter. There is a variety of texts which do that (Smith).

There's little variety, however, in the various texts at a given level. Here is one professor, for example, comparing two texts used for the introductory physics courses:

> The book we used to use was Resnick and Halliday. That's the one that I used when I was an undergraduate. Like I said, the material [in the new textbook, Ohanion] is all the same. In fact, if you look at all of those books, they might as well have been copied from one another. He tries to make his examples interesting. And his problems are more interesting. Instead of a block sliding down an inclined plane, the question is about some car skidding off of a racetrack. He puts real numbers in. The problems are more fun to work, even though you're working exactly the same problem (Slemp).

Dr Slemp's comments point to another critical feature of textbooks in physics. Up until now I've been talking about how the standardized, demodalized form in which the texts are written allows physics education to be spatially integrated across schools, departments and laboratories spanning the globe. But if physics textbooks are representational technologies for solidifying a dense social space across physically distanced settings and practices (if 'facts' are a good medium for connecting practices), textbooks are also sites for producing particular representations of space-time. By that I mean that physics textbooks are components of practices for mobilizing the physical world in textual form, and ultimately reconstructing it in representational space-times accessible only through texts or machinery for inscription: frictionless planes, perfect harmonic oscillators, 'invisible' particles and waves, and so on. We can get a general sense of how these practices developed within the recursive curriculum by briefly tracing changes in textbook treatments of physical phenomena.

Enrolling the World in Physics

Just as students were enrolled in the actor-network of physics, so were worldly phenomena. In the textbooks for the first courses in the physics sequence, the spaces of the physics textworld were initially described by analogy or contrast with the 'everyday', non-physics world. Consider this passage from an early chapter in the first mechanics textbook:

> Everyday experience suggests that a force — a push or a pull — is needed to keep an object moving at constant velocity. For example, if the wind pushing a sailboat suddenly dies out, the boat will coast along for some distance, but it will gradually slow down, stop, and remain stopped until a new gust of wind comes along. However, what actually slows down a sailboat is not the absence of a propulsive force, but, rather, the presence of friction forces. Under ideal frictionless conditions a body in motion would continue to move forever (Ohanian, 1985, p. 91).

The text starts us in a familiar space, the world of sailboats, but it redefines that space for us — explaining what 'really' slows the boat down — by defining the action in terms of a new entity: friction. Then we're told what would happen in an ideal space — a representation of space that can't be found 'out there', but that exists in the textworld. No equations, diagrams, or illustrations accompany this passage. The everyday analog — the sailboat — is like a model that we can use to make sense of the physics. We remain oriented in the familiar space of everyday practice, but everyday practice has been 'problematized' — given a specialized identity accessible only through the obligatory passage point of physics' representations of space.

By contrast, in a passage that occurs much later in the same text, references to 'everyday' objects play a very different role:

> Consider a tightly stretched elastic string, such as a long rubber cord. If we snap one end of the string back and forth with a flick of the wrist, a disturbance travels along the string. Figure 15.1 [not included] shows in detail how such a travelling disturbance comes about. The string may be regarded as a row of particles joined by small, massless springs. When we jerk the first particle to one side, it will pull the second particle to the same side, and this will pull the third, etc. If we then jerk the first particle back to the original position, it will pull the second particle back, and this will likewise pull the third. As the motion is transmitted from one particle to the next particle, the disturbance propagates along the row of particles. Such a disturbance is called a wave pulse (Ohanion, 1985, p. 369). [author amendment]

Here we see an 'interessement': the physics actor-network creates a barrier between the physical phenomena it defines and alternative defining networks. This passage is comprehensible *only* in terms of the discipline's representations of space. Although the passage supplies a specific 'everyday' image for the reader it's quickly clear that instead of a 'long rubber cord' (a phenomenon that could be enrolled in various non-physics representations of space) we're dealing with 'a row of particles joined by small, massless springs'. Rather than 'showing' this particle row, a diagram creates it: we would have no clear way of imagining such an 'object' without something like the diagram, and the rest of the paragraph makes little sense unless one can see or has seen similar diagrams.

If such scientific diagrams, as Lynch (1988) suggests, 'create the impression that the objects or relations they represent are *inherently* mathematical' (p. 169), then it's a small but consequential step to dispense with such diagrams and operate primarily in mathematical terms. This is the principal means through which phenomena are 'enrolled' — their identities stabilized through alliances — in the physics actor-network. Consider this introduction to the 'wave pulse' in a text for a third-year course in 'modern physics':

> Another familiar phenomenon not describable by a single travelling wave is that of a pulse, such as a sudden noise, a flip of one end of a long string, or the brief opening of a shutter in front of a light source. The main characteristic of a pulse is that of localization in time and space. A wave of a single frequency and wavelength such as any of those of Eqs. (5–10) has *no* localization in time or space. In order to describe a pulse, a group of waves of different frequencies and wavelengths must be taken. The range of wavelengths or frequencies needed depends on the extent of the space (or time) of the pulse. In general, if the extent in space, delta x, is small, the range of wave

numbers delta k must be large. The mathematics of representing arbitrarily shaped pulses by sums of sine or cosine functions involves Fourier series and Fourier integrals (Tipler, 1969, p. 201).

Even diagrams are no longer sufficient to formulate the phenomena; the 'objects' must be represented in mathematical equations. The paragraph still begins with the 'everyday world' but only to undercut our common experience of it: a sudden noise, the flip of a long string, the brief opening of a light shutter, are described as belonging to a *single* class of entities within the representational space of physics. Students are no longer dealing with entities constituted through the familiar material spatial practices of everyday activity: the entities have an identity only within the discipline's representations of space. They have been 'enrolled' in the physics actor-network, just as the students were.

Textbooks as Engines of Instruction

I don't want to go too far, however, talking about textbooks without considering how they are used. From my perspective as an outsider textbooks seem to tie together distant programs and departments and formulate a distinctive representational space-time. What professors and students actually do with the texts is another matter. Even given the demodalized formulation of the text statements there is still room for different appropriations of the texts by professors using them to teach courses, and for divergent readings by the students in the courses. If the texts are to be useful in holding networks together in a stable configuration and keeping activity 'on-track', then the representations in the texts have to be remobilized in a variety of ways.

The most obvious mobilizations are the professors' lectures over the subject matter in the text. As Traweek (1988) has noted, in both Japan and America the textbook is the principal engine of instruction in undergraduate physics education:

> Physics is introduced first to the undergraduate in a textbook. The instructors, who are presented as experts on physics (although not specialists in all subfields simultaneously), explain the material in the textbook. Students are given 'problem sets' to solve in order to demonstrate their comprehension of the material (Traweek, 1988, p. 76).[6]

The physics professors I talked to saw themselves following the textbooks closely in their sequencing and coverage of topics. 'The table of contents . . .' one professor noted 'would pretty well be a syllabus'. Another explained:

> I would say in general I do tend to follow the book, because I have found the students — well, in the first place, very few of them take good notes. So if I don't follow the book they have nothing to study

for a test. And I think it's the responsibility of the faculty to select books that are similar to what they're going to teach in the course. I also have seen studies which indicate that the students learn little from the lecture to begin with. So I've realized that most of what I'm doing is simply trying to explain to the better students some of the finer points and trying to help the weak students overcome the difficult parts (Morton).

Faculty allowed textbooks to define the subject matter and pedagogy of the courses they taught partly because the subject matter was considered 'dead', 'classical' material unrelated to the issues they dealt with in their research. Moreover, since teaching assignments were made by a departmental committee and changed from year to year, faculty had no personal investment in particular courses, and did not teach them frequently enough to develop distinctive approaches to the subject matter. Instead, most professors followed the textbooks and monitored and imitated the practices of others who were teaching or had taught the same courses. One professor compared himself in this way to another professor who'd taught the same book:

I made my students work more problems, and I think my tests were slightly harder. But we covered, to within 40 or 50 pages, the same parts of the same book and the students would see a difference only in that perhaps they would say one instructor was easier. But the topics covered would be much the same (Wilson).

It appears paradoxical, given this subservience to the text, that for students courses varied radically depending on who taught them. Paul, who called the professor just quoted 'horrible, beyond belief', argued that:

You can have the identical course and have different instructors, and they're almost completely different courses. Even though I don't put a lot of emphasis on what an instructor says, it's just, it depends on whether you have some idiot bellowing out some kind of drool up there at the front of the room, or somebody who's really competent and can really show you some interesting mental connections.

Paul was one of the students who worked alone instead of in a study group, but on this point his perceptions were shared by other students (though they tended to use less colurful language): the texts and content might be standardized and rigidly sequenced, but lectures were not. Although students claimed that professors just 'wrote the book to us' (Bob) in 'really boring' lectures (Alice), the professors obviously did not and could not have reproduced the books exactly in their lectures. Instead, they mobilized the forms embodied in the texts — the equations and diagrams. They temporalized and respatialized the static text landscapes, transformed them into tours.

Mobilizing the Textbook: Lectures

As representational organizations of space-time, physics textbooks presented students with complete 'terrains' described in explicit, non-modalized terms. To do physics was, for students, to chart journeys through these textual landscapes. Lectures, to follow the metaphor, were like guided tours through the terrain. If the textbooks mobilized physics in a stable form by deleting mention of agency, actions, and the antecedents of actions, it was through the re-insertion of such modalities, the reconstruction of textbook 'facts' in narratives, that the physics 'in' the textbooks was used to bind together courses and class sessions within a course. Lectures described the kinds of journeys that were feasible through the representational space, which were worth taking, and how one might negotiate them.

We can begin to get a sense of this 'modalization' of textbooks by considering a couple of pages in the textbook (Crawford, 1968) for the third course in the physics sequence, Waves. The book section is labelled 'Example 10: Two coupled LC circuits' and consists of a small quantity of text, eight equations, and one diagram.

These passages, which students encountered in the second semester of their second year in college, are framed almost entirely in demodalized, disciplinary representations of space-time. The author begins by presenting a 'system' in terms of a diagram of two coupled LC circuts, a highly formulaic representation of a kind that students had become acquainted with in their Introductory Electricity and Magnetism course. The section begins:

> Let us find the equations of 'motion' — motion of the change in this case. The electromotive force (emf) across the left-hand inductance is $L\, dI/dt$. A positive charge Q_1 on the left-hand capacitory gives an emf $C^1 Q_1$ that tends to increase I. (with our sign conventions) . . . (Crawford, 1968, p. 27–8).

In this fashion the diagram is translated into the more manipulable representational format of equations. The text then directs us to 'express the configuration of the system in terms of currents rather than charges' by differentiating and using conservation of charge to simplify portions of the equation to produce 'coupled equations of motion'. (It's assumed that these equations have a recognizable shape for the students). The normal modes are given, and the text section ends with a paragraph that links the example to other examples in the text and foreshadows issues to be discussed later in the book.

As written, this book section is like a piece of road map that shows how different routes link, which exits are available, and how different points in the terrain can be connected. What it lacks is any hint of why the routes exist and why one should want to go from one place to the next. Agency and action have been excised, and students alone lacked resources to reintroduce them. Instead, they had to draw on the problems in the book, their fellow students, and, the resource with which I begin, the lectures of their professors.

The lecture I'll examine here is by the professor most highly regarded by the students I interviewed, Dr Smith. Some, as I've already suggested, did little more than parrot the book, but the best narrativized the content and reintroduced some elements of agency and action into the demodalized text. The lecture segment described below, which is taken from the third course in the curriculum, Waves, deals with topics very close to those dealt with in the book section discussed above.

In beginning the lecture, Dr Smith did not explicitly orient the students to any section of the text. Instead, connections between lecture and text were implied by the use of similar diagrams and equations, and the content of both were linked to previous subject matter (the motion of coupled springs and masses) by the introduction of an agent:

> Smith began by suggesting that when God made the universe, 'he got lazy' and instead of inventing new rules for different forms of phenomena, made very different kinds of phenomena abide by the same rules. Thus electromagnetic systems operate in the same ways as the mechanical systems (the springs and masses) that the class had been dealing with up to this point.

While the invocation of God was a great rarity in physics discourse, it served a double function here. First, it supplied a reason — 'nature' — for the identical mobilizations of two (apparently) very different physical systems. It told the students that the identity was a reflection of 'the way things are' rather than an analytical convenience or a social convention. Second, this kind of explanation set up a boundary condition on the discussion: there could be no explanation or discussion of 'why' mechanical and electromagnetic systems were describable with the same formulation: it was simply a function of nature, of God's will. Having framed the lecture in this way, Smith could then proceed with the narrative formulation of the LC circuit. He began by drawing an 'example' on the board:

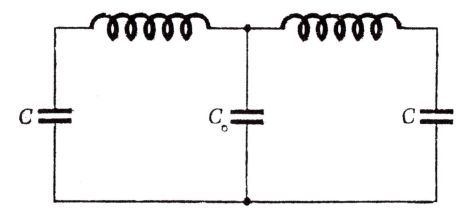

Diagrams such as this one (or the more detailed ones in the text) bundled together a set of representations. Making sense of them presupposed that students were not only familiar with those representations but with this particular way of connecting them. Thus even though the students had encountered such diagrams in their previous course (Introductory Electricity and Magnetism) Smith's first step was to see if they could 'read' it properly:

'What's "C" mean to you?' Smith asked. One student answered: 'charge'. 'Charge?' Smith responded, 'C means charge to you?' Another student tried an answer: 'storage of charge?'.

Not getting the answer he wanted, Smith began to create a narrative to lead the students through the representations implicit in the diagram. He began by shifting the focus of the lecture from the diagram to an 'everyday' object — to formulate a recognizable physical analog of the system described in the diagram. He began by:

picking up a flat, unfolded piece of aluminum foil, 'suppose I give you this piece of aluminum foil', Smith said, 'and let's say there's an electrical energy source in the corner of the room and electricity is fantastically expensive right now', and I say, 'okay, you can take this piece of foil and put all the charge you want on it, take all you want. Now, what's to stop you from becoming rich?'

Although the lecture was formulated in a questioning style, the class was large (about 70 students) and Smith didn't wait for answers. Having introduced an 'everyday', concrete example, he now began to encode it back into the representational system of physics.

Smith explained that as the charge was increased, the voltage would go up, and the stored energy would dissipate. 'Now', Smith asked, 'what if I wadded the foil up in a ball, or rolled it into a cylinder, how would that affect the process?' It would, he explained, produce a different voltage for the same charge. As the shape, the geometry, changes, the capacitor (and this, he explained, is what 'C' stands for) changes. Smith wrote the equation describing this relationship and explained that in the example given above, you want more charge per voltage:

$$C = \Psi/V$$

'So', Smith continued, 'if the system has a particular Ψ, its voltage is':

$$V_1 = \Psi/C$$

Smith then talked about what this meant in terms of coloumbs and joules.

We have gone from the diagram 'back' to the aluminum foil and then back to the diagram and the 'exotic' phenomena embodied in it (capacitors, voltage, etc.). The diagram has been 'modalized', inserted into a narrative that supplied an agent and actions that gave us a 'reason' for the diagram. That is, rather than simply defining 'C' Smith told a story that illustrated a use of the diagram. Using another everyday phenomenon as illustration, Smith repeated this kind of back and forth movement through the representational space:

> Smith then asked 'Historically, how did conductors come about? What was an early conductor?' Again, he provided the answer: The lightening rod.[7] Its top was a sharp point, and this meant [Smith drew the top of the rod and the lines of force] that when lightning struck it, the field created at the point was so strong that it ionized the air, pulling the negative charges out of the air and neutralizing the negative charges in the roof of the house:

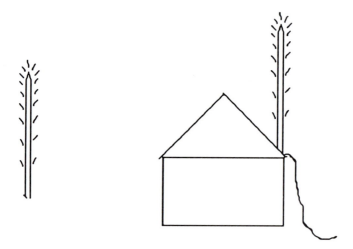

> This created a small, safe discharge. The rods themselves were connected to the earth (grounded) with a copper pipe (an excellent conductor), so that the charge would travel down the copper and be neutralized in the earth. What was discovered, however, was that sometimes, instead of following the copper to the earth, the current would 'jump' off the wire, onto the roof.

Having once again introduced a narrative, Smith then drew another, more schematic diagram, shifting the focus from the 'everyday' analog (the lightning rod) and onto a representation and a phenomenon imported from the representational space of physics:

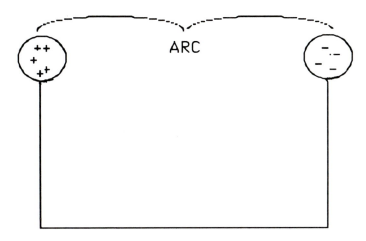

Why would there be arcs between the charged balls, Smith asked, instead of a flow of current through the copper wire? 'It's not simple DC resistence', Smith pointed out, and he went on to explain that the person who discovered this determined that the wire must have a property related to changes in the current. The wire is an 'inductor', the current building up in a loop produces a magnetic field and changing current produces an EMF, and changes the voltage. The field times the area of the wire equals the 'flux' (or the number of field lines). Flux is proportional to current: $\phi \alpha I$. And if we use L to represent a constant, the inductor, we get the equation:

$$\phi = LI$$

For voltage we get these equations:

$$V_L = Ld = \frac{d\phi}{dt} = \frac{LdI}{dt}$$

Smith reminded the students that they worked this out for solinoids, single loops, etc. in their previous physics course, Introductory Electricity and Magnetism. He mentioned Faraday's role in the discovery of these relationships, and pointed out that industrialization as we know it wouldn't have been possible without an understanding of these processes. Then returning to the initial example, Smith wrote the equations for the system and went on to find the modes, working through the details in more depth than the book had provided.

The class segment I've described illustrates two central features of physics lectures. First, Smith emphasized the connections among phenomena made by the book (for example, between springs-and-masses systems and LC circuits) and, when students had trouble with the 'abstract' representations in the text, he strategically shifted to more familiar, everyday representations. Second, and more importantly, he reorganized the content of the textbook into a collection of brief narratives. Instead of going through it section by section, he focused on particular points and illustrations and showed actual pathways through the myriad possible connections and routes in the text. As Karl's description of Smith's teaching suggests, instead of having to memorize the entire road atlas, students could focus on particular kinds of journeys:

> He would take ideas and make them quite clear, without making you feel slow. [pause] I guess for one thing he went through the course and took out all of the very important critical points, and he would introduce critical issues and introduce them in so many ways that finally you understood it completely. And so you didn't have to learn absolutely all the side issues. All you had to really learn were a few critical points and everything else was quite clear after that, because you just put it in terms of some fundamental concept. And the whole course came out (Karl).

In lectures like this one, then, professors took the virtual landscapes of the textbooks and transformed them into real-time journeys accomplished through the use of diagrams and mathematics: they mobilized the equations in the textbooks into a visual format that the students could, in turn, remobilize in their lecture notes.

Mobilizing the Lecture: Taking Notes

To get a sense of lectures from the students' perspective, we have to look at the physical organization of the lecture. The introductory, lower level courses for freshmen and sophomores (such as the one from which the excerpt given above was taken) were taught in a room in one of the older buildings on the campus, several blocks from the main physics building (the rest of the building was used exclusively by departments other than physics). This 'physics theatre' was designed for large lectures and demonstrations and had well over 100 seats stacked in sharply angled rows. Rather than a podium the teacher had a long lab table on which to set up demonstrations. A television mounted high to the side of the chalkboards and a projection booth at the back of the theatre were also used occasionally for demonstrations.

For the lectures, there were three levels of sliding chalkboards rising from waist level to the high ceiling. When one board was filled with equations and diagrams, the professor pushed it up (rather than erasing it) and continued his exposition on a new board. This allowed him to develop carefully and explicitly equations and their derivations for the students and to show their applications by working example problems. It also gave the students time to copy the board, to write it down in their notes.

The initial space of physics education was thus organized as a visual arena for faculty performances. The professor's work was the visual focus of the setting. He was physically set off from the students at the bottom of the room, surrounded by the paraphernalia of visual display. The major focus of vision was a system of moving, overlapping chalkboards that allowed him to 'save' visual representations and refer back to earlier equations and derivations during later parts of the lecture. There were also less frequently used demonstration apparatuses that allowed the creation of visual displays designed to break down and restructure students' everyday habits of seeing: illustrating the superposition principle, for example, by setting two hacksaw blades held on end in vices vibrating out of phase, then cutting the lights and turning on a strobe-lamp at the proper frequency to show them moving 'together'.

Students were spectators in this setting. At a period when physics accounted for only a small proportion of their coursework, the room was a special setting for undercutting their everyday practices of ordering the visual world. By the time students reached their third and last course in the physics theatre — Waves — this visual practice was pushed to its extreme. As Lem explained it, Waves was the course where one became acquainted with 'new' sorts of phenomena like oscillating systems that were 'unfamiliar' from everyday life and from the introductory courses:

> It expands your horizons, you might say. You get used to not working with dolls and rocks and bricks and cars, you get used to things that are not distinct in themselves. Like a wave on a string is not a graspable object. It's something that's transient. And you get used to working with things that change in time and in position. They're fleeting, they're not always there. They're constantly moving and changing. It's not like 'throw a rock this far, boom, it lands, how far away did it land?' You can ask more interesting questions about waves.

Courses like Waves began to introduce students to the representational space, peculiar to physics, that contained phenomena not found outside in the everyday world. That is, students became participants in distributed systems, unlike those they could participate in outside the program, that constituted the physical world in the particular way of physics. Demonstrations were used much more sparingly (films never in my fieldwork), and even then required a certain kind of 'reading' to be made sensible. A row of steel balls suspended in a frame from stiff rods and connected with springs could represent certain kinds of 'wave' motions, but the semiotic character of the demonstration had changed from the earlier courses. There, a hockey puck gliding, seemingly without deceleration over a plane of dry ice, produced a direct sign (hockey puck) — referent (law of motion) link. In later courses, however, a demonstration might consist of steel balls and springs (sign) linked to their referent (simple harmonic motion) through the medium of a symbol (the wave). The observable was no longer simply portrayed in a different fashion, it was made to stand for something else. The physics theatre had become not just a setting for instruction, but a place where a different order of seeing was required — one which looked through everyday appearances for the flat inscriptions hidden beneath. Within this setting, students took notes diligently.

> Generally I'll copy anything that's written on the board. Most of the professors that I've had, the information that is most critical is the things that they write down on the board. I write down some of the things that they say, but usually what they're saying is mainly just an explanation of what they've put up on the board. So you're writing what's on the board and then their explanation of what they've written up there. Or if it's for a certain type of problem, if I'm able, then I'll write down instructions on how to do the problem, or clarifications on why you work a problem a certain way. It's generally you write down about everything that you can (Bob).

> I take down most of what the professor will say, and all the details of the proofs, unless it's one that I happen to know is in the book. Something like that. Or one that I know I can work out myself later on. And so it's anything at all that I could possibly want later. That's how I think about it but I always end up deciding that I would want everything (Karl).

If you were to peer over students' shoulders during a lecture, as I often did, you would see sheets of equations and diagrams with very few words on them — nothing like my notes quoted earlier in this chapter. Part of the reason for this was the pace of lecturing and its visual organization. In courses where the professor's words carried the main informative burden (such as some of the business courses described in later chapters), students did not need to watch the board constantly: they watched the professor, and when he signalled that something was worth noting they could keep their heads down writing. In physics, by contrast, students had to move their eyes back and forth from the board to the notepaper (it was impossible to get the math down right without watching what you were doing) and I found it physically very difficult — even as an experienced notetaker — to get down anything more than the equations on a page. Even in this I had greater problems than the physics students who, so to speak, knew the basic 'grammar' of the 'language' the professor was speaking and could better anticipate what was to come.

Thus when I sat in the physics theatre I found myself torn between wanting to simply sit back and watch the board work and concentrate on the professors' explanations (which usually allowed me to follow what was going on and make sense of the physics), and frantically trying to write everything down and leaving class unsure what it had been about. The students, by contrast, weren't simply following the professors passively, they were running ahead of them, trying to anticipate what would be written on the board:

> If [the professor] says, you know, 'let's try and do it this way', I'll go ahead and I'll work a little bit ahead of him in my head and just kind of write it out and see if what I'm doing is the same thing as he's doing. It's more of a comparative to see if my, if the way I am thinking about it is the way you should be (Mick).

> It's important to me to try to keep a little bit ahead of the professor rather than just mindlessly copying what's on the board and not picking it up. And so this means I try to stay a step ahead of him and this also means I get sidetracked and go off solving my own little problems. But you take notes of the basics of what he's putting up on the board, how to do it. But then more importantly you're doing asides. All of the good physics students that I work with do the same thing, you say, 'ah, this is why this works' . . . You're trying to anticipate what it is, where he's going, and what the next step is going to be (Arnold).

> You try to do more than follow along. If they're doing a proof, you try to anticipate what the next step is going to be. . . . It's always sitting there looking for questions and seeing if he's answering them or if you can answer them (Alice).

Instead of simply reducing and compressing the course into a mobile product (as management students did in their notetaking), the experience of taking notes was as (or more) important for physics students than the content of the notes. In taking notes the students were interacting with the professors' performances at the same time as they were reproducing them in immutable and mobile forms on notebook paper. If the textbooks were like maps and charts, the notes were like nautical logs of journeys that students could accumulate, compare, and analyze in a single forum — the study group sessions.

That professors 'wrote the book' on the chalkboard, taught straight out of the book, or 'explained' the book, was thus not obvious to the students as the lectures unfolded. As Debbie explained, the realization of these identities was an accomplishment, a discovery:

> I take the notes in class, listen to what he says — then I go read the textbook and then I go back to the notes and realize that it's the same thing (laughs). . . . I never, say, reread the book for a liberal arts course. [. . . In physics] I really go through it carefully because, especially our physics books now in the upper levels, they don't work out everything for you. They leave it for the reader. And this reader goes through and proves it to herself, because it really helps in actually working

problems, or working on a test, to know where the background formulas came from. So I go through it very carefully. [. . .] And then I do the homework (Debbie).

The expository sections of the textbooks were opaque, complicated, and students could not rely on them as the primary sources of enlightenment (those who tried failed):

I don't do readings because textbooks put me to sleep. And I'm not kidding, it's almost like a phobia or a mental block. I start reading a textbook and I fall asleep. Within 20 minutes. It's just too dry. I don't learn well from books because I like to be able to ask questions. If I'm reading along and I read something that doesn't quite make sense to me, and no matter how hard I think about it, for some reason I'm just not looking at it right or whatever the reason that it doesn't make sense, everything they base on that no longer makes sense. If you don't understand why the building stands up, then you'll always look at it in awe. The whole thing just doesn't seem like it should be there. And so that gives me a real problem (Lem).

You can't read an atlas as you would a novel. Instead, students relied on the lectures to make the texts sensible — and on the end-of-chapter problems that served as the focus of their homework.

Mobilizing the Textbook and the Lecture Notes: Homework Problems

If the textbooks were like atlases that constituted the landscapes they described, and lectures were like narratives of journeys through those landscapes, then the text 'problems' were like outings or field trips. They keyed students to how their textbooks and notes might be used:

I tend to read textbooks backwards. In other words I look at the problem, and then I see what the textbook has to say that applies to the problem, and then I work the problems; and go backwards. I'll read a chapter through, but it really doesn't help you. I mean what you 'should' do is you read a chapter and then you get to the problem and then you solve it; but if you read the problem first you know what you're looking for, what kind of ideas you need to understand (Alice).

Problems were also the key tasks by means of which students were evaluated. Homework problems usually counted for 20 to 30 per cent of a course grade, and the tests that accounted for the remainder consisted of problems like those in the homework. This homegeneity in the task structure of courses meant that students studied, and studied for tests, not by trying to memorize formulas, definitions, or concepts, but by exercising their abilities to move through textworlds in the form of problem-solving. As we saw in the last chapter this was a collective experience:

> You take the notes and read the text and I make an outline of what it is that we've learned and try to put all these notes and scribblings into some logical order. And then you just work problems and work problems and work problems. And argue about them with you classmates (Arnold).

> But in most of the classes, the notes are — you read through the chapter maybe, again before you take the test, and you definitely go through all of the notes and make sure you understand everything in the notes, and then you also use the notes to help in problem-solving. Because most of the good professors will give a lot of examples of different types of problems, so you'll be able to do the homework, and so when you're working the homework you can look back at the examples they've done in class and use the notes that way too (Bob).

Students took advantage of the standardization of textbooks in the discipline to use non-assigned textbooks as sources of study problems. These additional texts did not describe or include different things; they simply provided additional maps of the textspace:

> Almost everybody reads things from outside the assigned homework, solves problems. . . . There's stuff from the library, or books just purchased — for instance, the Feynman lectures — I think everybody who's serious about getting out of here owns the Feynman lectures and uses them as a resource. [. . .] They introduce the same material from a different point of view and give problems to work (Arnold).

The additional problems these texts provided, like problems generally, posed short journeys though those regions, they gave the students opportunities to 'get from one place to another', in Feynman's (1965) words. Thus students actively looked for problems and used them as frameworks around which to organize their study group activities:

> All of the problems in a physics textbook are never assigned. So there's always a lot there. Also, a lot of times, especially in quantum mechanics, the teacher will bring other problems, and will leave parts of the proof up to you to do, as an exercise. And the other place is, a couple of friends and I sit around and ask each other about — make up problems. Sometimes they relate to class and sometimes just for the fun of it (Alice).

This semester we find it extremely useful to do [the problems] in groups . . . you set up the problem, and usually there'll be at least one person in there who'll say, 'well, I think we can start in this way', and if, you know, if we start working on that tangent and nothing works, we'll say, 'well, I guess that's wrong, let's try something else'. It's mostly trial and error and practice. . . . It helps because different people key on different things when you read a chapter or when you understand problems (Kelly).

We work on something until we come to a problem. One of us will have a problem on it. And then we'll ask each other if we know how to do it, or 'what did you think about this?' and then we'll usually — usually there's someone who has some kind of idea on it, and one of us will go up to the board and start writing out our ideas on the board, and then everyone who's having a problem with it will sit there and work on it together (Bob).

Participating in the representational organization of space-time of the textbooks and problems was something students could not easily do alone. They needed textbooks, pencils, paper, a room with a chalkboard (not easy to find in physics buildings, the group sessions would move from week to week as space was available) — and they needed each other. As Alice explained:

I very rarely do homework assignments completely on my own. It's a very work together climate. . . . When you get stuck you don't just sit there and mull over it. And you don't have to run to find a professor every time you get stuck. The other thing is that they tend to point out your weaknesses. You know, Mike knows this and I don't. So I guess I need to study this more. Four heads is better than one. Talking about physics is a real important part of it. If you just try to always think about it or write about it I don't think you ever know what you knew. You need to talk about it, you need to be able to put it into words, what you know. Because if you can't, then you really can't understand it. And so working with other people forces you to put it into words, to say what you think, to say why you think your answer is right and his is wrong. . . . We work, just going through, basically solving problems. And we would just take turns. Each getting up to the blackboard and writing the next equation, and arguing about why things are, and why we believe the answer is this, and there were a lot of things that we found we didn't understand and we argued through some of them.

If the program's material organization of space-time compressed students into groups, then the problem format provided the medium and the trigger for group interaction. Although some authors have pointed to the emphasis on

problem-solving as the generative force behind the development of disciplinary 'mental sets' or 'Einstellungen' in fields such as physics (Kuhn, 1963), I
think it more fruitful to say that problem-solving is an exercise in mobilizing
phenomena and producing disciplinary representational spaces. This relieves
us of the dubious cognitivist assumptions behind the idea of 'mental sets' and
allows us to ask two important questions: why was problem-solving the principal pedagogical medium in physics education, and why did social, group-
efforts became the dominant format for working problems?

Mobilizations of the Physical World within Disciplinary Space

As we go 'further' (in a social, not just physical sense) from the center of a
network (such as the practices of professional physicists), more and more
mobile and immutable representations are required to bind the network together. In physics education each mobilization was accomplished through a
stripping away of 'context': the textbooks mobilized equations by stripping
away the context of practice, the lectures mobilized the textbooks by stripping
away the context they supplied, the students' note-taking mobilized the lectures by stripping away the words of the professors, and the homework problems mobilized everything by stripping away all except the equations and the
diagrams: the basic building blocks of 'reality' in the representational space of
physics.

This relentless reduction of the world to textual forms allowed students to
construct linkages among the courses in the recursive curriculum:

> It's really kind of funny, because as one is taking a class — at least I
> always tend to feel that it's removed from every other thing. It's very
> specific. And then you'll be taking another class, and then and only
> then do you start seeing the overlap, and once you get really into
> things, it's all a big continuum (Paul).

> After you've taken a course and you're on to the next level, you see
> how that course really helps you to get to where you are now. And
> you do that each step of the way. As you're actually taking it you're
> basically trying to get through the course, pass, get a grade, and
> unfortunately I find that I don't understand it as much while I'm taking
> it as I do *afterwards* — when I've seen everything, then I see how it
> all sort of fits together and intertwines (Debbie).

Each 'exposure' to a topic across the courses and years re-inscribed the
topic in ever more mobile, mathematized forms (forming what Latour calls a
'cascade of representations'). This mobilization through increasing 'formalization' made it possible to bind together the various courses of the curriculum

in a way that connected them in turn to the heterogeneous spaces of the disciplinary network. Latour (1987) suggests that formalization is a way for disciplinary networks to stabilize their control over a region of practice (to impose or maintain a spatio-temporal structure):

> When people wonder how 'abstract' geometry or mathematics may have some bearing on 'reality', they are really admiring the *strategic position* taken by those who work inside the centers on forms of forms. They should be the weakest since they are the most remote (as it is often said) from any 'application'. On the contrary, they may become the strongest by the same token as the centers end up controlling space and time: they design networks that are tied together in a few obligatory passage points. Once every trace has been not only written on paper, but rewritten in geometrical form, and rewritten in equation form, then it is no wonder that those who control geometry and mathematics will be able to intervene almost anywhere. The more 'abstract' their theory is, the better it will be able to occupy centers inside the centers. . . . The more heterogeneous and dominating the centers, the more formalism they will require simply to stay together and maintain their imperium (p. 245).

As the mobilizations of the equations became more formal (to bind the large network) group activity became important precisely because the 'empirical' world had been factored out of the equations. Students moving through the curriculum gradually lost access to everyday, familiar referents; they were forced to draw upon each other to formulate 'abstract' referents (phenomena existing in physics' representational organization of space-time).

Kuhn (1970) put his finger on the technology of physics education — the problem — but missed its function in suggesting that:

> Doing problems is learning consequential things about nature. In the absence of such exemplars, the laws and theories he [the student] has previously learned would have little empirical impact. . . . The student discovers, with or without the assistance of his instructor, a way to see his problem as like a problem he has already encountered. Having seen the resemblance, grasped the analogy between two or more distinct problems, he can interrelate symbols and attach them to nature in the ways that have proved effective before. The law-sketch, say $f = ma$, has functions as a tool, informing the student what similarities to look for, signalling the *gestalt* in which the situation is to be seen. The resultant ability to see a variety of situations as like each other, as subjects for $f = ma$ or some other symbolic generalization, is, I think, the main thing a student acquires by doing exemplary problems, whether with a pencil and paper or in a well-designed laboratory (pp. 188, 189).

Kuhn's cognitivist reading ignores the social nature of problem work (learning to 'see' connections among problems was a social, discursive accomplishment), but even more problematic is the notion that students were 'attaching' something to nature. 'Nature', at least the way we constitute it in everyday practice, was precisely what had been purged from the problems. Indeed, it's not clear that this level of problem work was even relevant to the representational practices of physicists. Paul, the only student among those I interviewed with experience in a major research lab, observed that:

> Academic problem-solving . . . is so completely removed from what you have to do, ultimately. I mean, you're never going to have to sit and figure out how a penny spins and show it mathematically. And on top of that, everything is set up for you. It's so completely orthogonal to real life situations.

If there was any 'nature' or 'empirical reality' to be found in the problem sets, it was a reality *constructed* by and in the practices of problem-solving. As Arnold explained, looking back from the perspective of a student near graduation, the introductory courses had provided:

> a better intuitive grasp for what's going on. By the time you've gotten into classical dynamics or classical electrodynamics the math is so powerful — it's just amazing to be able to solve these problems that you had to slave over in earlier courses just in one line. But if your only introduction to these concepts . . . is through this very powerful mathematics, you're going to lose touch with what's going on behind the math, with the physics. And so you develop, perhaps, your intuitive grasp of the real world in the introductory courses, as well as just an ability to comprehend this mathematics and apply it. . . . It's a levels process. In graduate school I'll take exactly the same thing [e.g., mechanics], except at a higher level of mathematics.

Comments like this illustrate the importance of 'intuition' and 'physicality' (both of which were accomplishments won through years of coursework) in the discourse of physics: they rooted physics in a 'real', objective world. As Alice's comments suggest, this sense of possessing a privileged access to the physical world was a constitutive element of being a physicist:

> You can't learn the higher mathematic content if you don't understand the principles behind it. . . . I mean, you have to keep a real good grasp on what is physical and what isn't, or else you'd be a mathematician.

But what does this discourse of 'physicality' entail? In Alice's account below, a 'chair' is no longer something you sit in, it has become an object in the representational space-time of physics:

When you take mechanics at the freshman level, you don't solve anything that's real. You're working with frictionless ropes and frictionless rods and frictionless pulleys — I mean massless rods — nothing is taking into account all of the little perturbations, the little things that make life interesting, and make a problem interesting. You can't, you know, solve what happens when you push on a chair. I mean a chair is a complicated object, it's not square, it's not spherical, it's not shaped like a rod.

What was 'physical' or 'intuitive' here were forms describable in mathematical terms. Mathematical formalization became the necessary bridge from the pre-physics notions of physicality that the students brought with them to the program to more 'abstract' disciplinary notions of 'concrete' reality. Karl explained this better than any of the other students I interviewed. He began by saying that he tried to keep everything grounded in a physical understanding:

When I study physics, what I like to be able to do is be able to reduce everything that I know down to a few concepts which make sense based on a physical level. So when I look at a step I like to be able to reduce it, to take that equation and understand what it's saying on a physical level.

But then he went on to explain what he meant by 'physical':

The framework that I've had has changed considerably from the time that I came in, especially when I got into my quantum mechanics classes, where a lot of things aren't physically interpretable, but what you do is start out with a set of abstract postulates and come up with it. So that was a very interesting idea — to have abstract postulates. I'm interested in math too, and that was very exciting to me, very interesting. I had a sudden realization that the physical postulates — the 'physical' postulates — were also abstract, that I just saw them, that was all (Karl).

This notion of 'abstract physicality' is widely accepted among physicists. The Physics Survey Committee (1972), for example, defended college physics programs from the charge that they over-emphasized the mathematics and turned 'students into mindless equation solvers':

One reason for this preoccupation with formalism is the fantastic growth of quantum mechanics and its impact on most of physics. But there is at least one other cause. To look at a problem from the proverbial, and somewhat subjectively defined, physical point of view may seem like the natural, innate, human approach, but actually it requires time, patience and experience to develop physical intuition. Although good teaching can help a student substantially in this process of maturing, there is no reason to discard the learning crutch provided by easy familiarity with formal manipulation. Excessive mathematization of the curriculum for its own sake is certainly undesirable, but the use of formalism is obviously to be encouraged whenever it can eliminate impediments to physical understanding (From Physics Survey Committee, 1972, p. 763).

This is a distinctive ontology, one in which mathematical formalization is necessary to eliminate the 'impediments', presumably common senuous experience, that hinder physical understanding. As students encountered the 'same' subject matter over and over, abstract formalisms became physical intuitions, the 'physical' became 'abstract'. It's as though the further one moves from everyday space into the space-time constituted in the representations, the closer one is said to move to reality, to nature. 'Nature' itself is that which connects heterogeneous spaces, and those connections are mathematical forms. As Feynman (1965) puts it: 'If you want to learn about nature . . . it is necessary to understand the language she speaks in. She offers her information only in one form: mathematics' (p. 58).

This did not mean, of course, that the students confused the everyday with the physics world, that Alice could no longer simply sit in chairs, or that Karl made no distinctions between cars on the street and elementary particles. The students moved through the representational spaces of physics as, and only as, components of 'distributed' actors that included other students as well as their professors, their textbooks, and their pencils and paper. The curriculum did not annihilate the everyday world, but it created a different 'real' world in representations of space.

As long as we deal with discrete 'local' phenomena, we can formulate them in concrete, modalized representations 'based on simple experience with everyday objects': 'pendulums', for example, to talk about simple motion, LC diagrams to talk about electricity (cf. Feynman, 1965, p. 127). When we want to examine many dispersed spaces and phenomena, however, it's necessary to represent them in forms that are mobile and unchanging. How to connect pendulums and circuits? Our everyday associations help little; it's difficult to visualize the two phenomena as one. But the connection is easily accomplished if we transform them into mathematical representations. An equation, as Latour (1987) puts it 'ties different things together and makes them equivalent' (p. 238). The more spaces we want to connect, the greater the 'range of phenomena' we bind, the more mathematically involved the representations become and the more problematic intuition based on everyday experience becomes.

But this was not the entire story. Physics students, somewhere in the course of their undergraduate studies, stopped focusing simply on the problem of mobilizing everyday phenomena — translating them into mathematical forms so that they could be connected to other mobilized phenomena — and instead began to work with representations that had become detached from phenomena — second-, third-, or nth-order mobilizations (Latour, 1987, pp. 243–4).

While it was important for the students initially to link equations to visual representations of physical systems such as circuits, after a point, like sailors operating far from shore, their primary media became the equations themselves. They followed the chain of mobilizations until the links themselves were all that remained in view, the initial anchorings had receded into the distance. Instead of functioning as models of physical systems, diagrams and other visual representations became partial illustrations of mathematized systems, and once into the quantum mechanics portion of the curriculum the phenomena students dealt with were no longer approachable except though the mathematized representational organization of space. Traweek (1988), in her study of high energy physicists,[8] describes them as building:

> an extreme culture of objectivity: a culture of no culture, which longs passionately for a world without loose ends, without temperament, gender, nationalism, or other sources of disorder — for a world outside *human* time and space (p. 162, emphasis added).

In the undergraduate physics program we can see the beginnings of the practices by means of which physicists move out of human, everyday bodily space-time, and into the textual space-time of the discipline. Just as the material organization of space-time in the program pressed students into groups and closed out outsiders, the representational organization of space-time connected students with a domain of practice inaccessible to outsiders. The trajectories of disciplinary practice lead almost exclusively toward a relatively few organized centers — research universities and laboratories — where powerful technologies of representation and construction mobilize the world in a form malleable to the discipline. The result is a tightly organized disciplinary actor-network, one in which people physically distant and never in face-to-face interaction can work together on specific mobilizations or constructions of the world (theories or experiments).

The mobilization and compression of the world into disciplinary spaces is not, however, the only way a discipline can constitute itself as a powerful actor-network. In the next two chapters I'll examine the management program as another way of educating practitioners for powerful disciplines, one which moves them along trajectories into loosely organized networks and mobilizes their practice in a very different fashion.

Notes

1   Actually, there were four iterations if they'd taken high school physics courses, which usually cover the same ground as the first two college courses, albeit in a

mathematically simplified form. Sharon Traweek (1988) suggests that this recursive curriculum reflects a strategic withholding of the 'truth' common to long novitiates. Students:

> learn that information taught at each state is often distorted or partial, a very rough approximation of the truth, which is to be disclosed at later stages. Novices are thought to be unsuited to a full disclosure of truth in these first years (p. 80).

As the text makes clear, I don't think this is the whole story (and for the faculty's part I think it was less an unwillingness to share the truth with entering students than the fact that 'the truth' as they understood it could only be expressed in terms not yet meaningful to students).

2   In any organizational field dominated by an oligopoly there are strong pressures for product standardization and homogeneity (cf. Peterson and Berger, 1975; Dimaggio and Powell, 1983). Since the textbook industry itself has an oligopical structure (Coser, Kadushin and Powell, 1982) there is a general pressure for the standardization of all texts in a given market area. In the case of physics — an oligopically structured discipline — these pressures seem to have produced a rigidity.

3   As Kuhn (1970) has observed, such a textualization of disciplinary practice is a common feature of science fields (or at least, we should qualify, their educational components):

> To an extent unprecedented in other fields, both the layman's and the practitioner's knowledge of science is based on textbooks and a few other types of literature derived from them (Kuhn, 1970, p. 137).

4   The top twenty graduate programs in the National Academy of Science (1983) rankings listed thirty-six texts in their descriptions of undergraduate preparation.

5   Few of the textbooks in use when I studied the program were under a decade old (in the undergraduate management program, by contrast, none of the textbooks was more than five years old).

6   Traweek goes on to analyze what she calls the 'subliminal' messages in a textbook, but does not examine how textbooks are read or used by students or faculty.

7   The 'lightning rod' example was a familiar trope in physics textbooks prior to World War II (e.g., Saunders, 1936, pp. 334–5).

8   Traweek's study shows some of the other practices — those of experimentalists working with experimental machinery — that constitute the space-time order of physics. Again, undergraduate programs are only a beginning; the students who graduate from them do not emerge as fully-fledged disciplinary practitioners.

Chapter 4

Constructing and Isolating Academic Space in Management

The student's career on campus is trivial as compared with future rewards and responsibilities, but given certain common conditions, his experiences are an unwitting preparation for the executive role. Years of 'education' have many implications for the type of student (a) who attends school with more vocational than intellectual purpose; (b) who wishes to participate widely on campus and yet craves good marks; and (c) who for these and other reasons is forced to budget his time (Dalton, 1958, p. 164).

The physics program's compression of space, exclusion of outsiders, and mobilizations of physical phenomena represent one example of how a 'science' begins to shape practitioners by connecting them to the world it constructs. In this chapter and the next I'll examine a very different way of producing social spaces and actor-networks: that of corporate enterprise, at least as it manifested itself in a management program that created an extensive but fragmented disciplinary space and mobilized social phenomena in bodily practices. Where the physics program pulled its students out of their bodies, the management program reconstructed and mobilized student bodies.

If the physics program was like a moving pathway shuttling students into discipline-specific material and representational organizations of space-time, the management program was more like a boundary that simultaneously defined and created points of passage between two regions: the academic world and the business world. It follows that the discussion of the management program and its students won't have the structure of the preceding chapters.

The material organization of space-time in the physics program gradually cut off physics students from other material spaces and separated them from students in other programs. The management program, by contrast, congregated students' coursework in the business school building by their third year, but allowed students from the different business programs to mingle with each other. Whereas physics students' coursework consumed their waking hours, the coursework in management was never so demanding as to occupy the majority of students' time outside the classroom.

The result in physics was the creation of a distributed actor, the problem-solving groups, that could sustain the massively reductive educational/textual space-time produced by the representational practices of the discipline. In the management program, by contrast, students intersected with large networks that expanded social space instead of compressing it. Instead of a dense social space that linked a small group of students together with strong ties, management students were tenuously linked by weak ties to a potentially enormous network of practitioners. These weak but highly extendable ties were fashioned through the bodily practices and styles of sociability that were part of the program's material production of space.

Reversing the order in which I dealt with the forms of spatial production in the physics program, I'll examine that material production of space-time and bodily practices in the next chapter and begin here with the representational production of space in the program. The reason is that the latter, which in physics was about mobilizing and compressing phenomena into disciplinary forms, merely produced two rigidly separated domains in the management program: a weak, subordinate 'academic' world defined by the representational practices of the business school, and a robust 'real world' defined by the material practices of the modern corporation. I want to show how this division was produced before examining how it connected students to domains of disciplinary practice.

Variable Points of Entry

In contrast to the 5,000 Bachelor's degrees awarded in physics each year in the US, about 190,000 Bachelor's degrees were awarded yearly in business at the time of this study, 17 per cent of them in management (Hugstad, 1983, pp. 42, 110).

As a field of practice, however, 'management' isn't just larger than physics, it's also more internally differentiated and more spatially dispersed (Whitley, 1984, describes it as a 'fragmented adhocracy'). The most prestigious business schools are graduate institutions that de-emphasize or don't offer undergraduate degrees in business fields. These graduate schools orient themselves towards producing workers for the growing managerial ranks of the modern corporation (Chandler, 1977). Other institutions, like the one I studied, have maintained specialized undergraduate majors while simultaneously building up their graduate programs (cf. Wheeler, 1966, pp. 62–4).

Although graduate and undergraduate programs have different goals and student clienteles, there is a tension between the two in institutions that contain both. At the university I studied, an ascendant faction of the management department's faculty concentrated on graduate education and felt that improving the reputation of the department meant de-emphasizing (or eliminating) the undergraduate program. 'We do not put a lot of emphasis on the undergraduate program', the new department chair told me:

> The widely-held philosophy in this department is that the students are better off getting more of a Liberal Arts education at the undergraduate level, with enough professional training so if that's their last degree then they are employable.[1]

Teaching responsibilities for the undergraduate courses had been shifted to a small group of older, tenured faculty, and a number of non-tenure track instructors (for the most part retired executives hired as adjuncts).[2]

One consequence of this situation was that, unlike physics, where shifting teaching assignments distanced professors from the content and facilitated a textbook-based standardization of the curriculum, undergraduate management faculty (including adjuncts) essentially 'owned' their courses, defined the content and function of the courses for themselves, and taught them year after year. This connected the undergraduate management program to its organizational field very differently than the physics program. The graduate component in management was oriented towards academia (in the PhD route) or the managerial ranks of national firms (in the MBA route), while the undergraduate component oriented itself toward the lower and mid-management ranks of regional enterprises,[3] many of them linked to the business school through alumni, corporate contributors and recruiters, or through the faculty who as consultants or former executives retained close ties to regional firms.

The result was that being an undergraduate management major seemed to mean little more than getting on any of a number of pathways that might lead to a good job in one of these regional firms after graduation. Students could step onto these pathways at various times in their college careers. There were not, as in the physics program, spatial and temporal boundaries limiting students' entry into the management program to an early stage in their academic careers. There was none of the progressive compression of spatial and temporal practices and social ties that characterized physics students' academic careers from high school onward.[4] Only one of the management students I interviewed, in fact, had decided to major in the field in high school. The others took advantage of the program's temporally loose course-taking requirements to move into it in the middle of their college careers.

By a 'loose' course structure I mean that although there were many required courses (see Appendix 1) there were few prerequisite restrictions on when they could be taken. This allowed students to compress required coursework into a minimal number of semesters: they could switch to business in their second or third years, choose management as a major their final year, and fit the courses into their schedules without great difficulty.

Some students, like Curtis, Joe and Jack, began college in programs with strong exclusionary pressures (in their case engineering, a program with deadly 'weed-out courses') and switched to management because of grade problems. Bart, for example, moved to management from the pre-dentistry program — which he'd only gone into in the first place because his girlfriend was a dental assistant — when second-year chemistry 'kicked [his] ass'. Business, too, had introductory, lower-division courses aimed at weeding out students: notoriously punative courses like economics and business mathematics. As Sheena recalled, her freshman economics class met at

> Nine o'clock in the morning Monday, Wednesday, and Friday. I'll never forget that class (laughs). He always talked to the chalkboard — always talked to the chalkboard. And, you know, it's one of those classrooms that goes straight up. I always sat at the back because I'd always come to the class a minute before the bell rang. And he locks the doors. If you're late you don't come in. If he forgets to lock one of the doors, 'cause there's two entrances, he yells at you and he will ask you to leave. You must pay attention, you must take notes, or else he'll ask you why you're not taking notes. If you fall asleep in class it's deadly. A few of us did that.

Courses like this, and the business school's minimal grade point average requirements (there were none in physics), winnowed the study body. Unlike physics, however, the goal was not to produce a small, highly-motivated cohort of students, but simply to reduce the very large number of students who wanted business degrees.[5]

The majority of students were not refugees, however. For some, like Delbert and Velma, the program was a fall-back when they found they wanted business degrees but didn't have an interest in any particular field. For other students such as Dell and Rhonda, both of whom were double-majoring in marketing, the management degree was simply a hedge against job shortages in their preferred field. This also indicated, of course, the students' flexibility or lack of commitment to a specific occupation. Dell, for example, liked marketing best, but was considering an internship in insurance underwriting on the advice of his girlfriend's boss (who was in the insurance field). Curtis wanted to work for a bank, but recognized that with the banking industry in a slump this might be impossible. Rhonda wanted to work in marketing for a major pharmeceutical corporation, but had discovered through contacts in the field (her father was a doctor) that they rarely hired employees directly out of college.

Finally, some students went into management simply because somebody suggested it to them. Clara, for example, majored in management because she'd read an article in *Working Women* magazine describing hospital administration as a growing field, not because she had any prior interest in management or hospitals. For Dorothy, the decision to major in management was:

> my father's choosing. . . . I wasn't sure what I wanted to do as a freshman, and my father said, why don't you do business, and so I said all right, and he said, why don't you get, quote, 'the easiest and most liberal degree you can get in the school of business' — which I believe to be management.

The choice of management as a major, then, in sharp contrast to physics, had little to do with the field itself. It was the product of expedience, the exclusion of alternatives, or the result of external direction or advice. It follows that the program itself was not defining identities and interests — it was not advancing a problematization — in the same fashion as the physics program. In the next chapter I'll suggest that the program *was* mobilizing students in a way that made them particularly 'suited' to the problematizations of a whole range of corporate actor-networks to whom they might be connected. Here, however, I want to note briefly one aspect of the different constructions of gender in the two programs.

Management students were drawn from a more diverse array of family backgrounds than physics students. Parents of the latter were college educated and for the most part employed in the corporate, academic, or government sectors of the economy. There were also working-class students in physics, while I never encountered them in management (although there are bound to have been some). Instead, the parents of the management students included small businessmen and lower-level managers as well as professionals, and their educational backgrounds were varied: some had not gone beyond high school.[6] It was the position of women in the two programs, however, that was most strikingly different.

In a sense, if physics was a prototypical 'male' program (part of a rigidly structured career sequence planned out years in advance), students' trajectories into the management major resembled the 'loose, episodic structures' that Dorothy Smith (1987, p. 66) says characterize women's lives, 'not so much a career as a series of contingencies, of accidents, so that I seem to have become who I am almost by chance' (p. 65). While 90 per cent of the physics majors were men, an equal number of men and women majored in management. While women are still disadvantaged in actual managerial practice (Kanter, 1977), several characteristics of the management program I studied opened it up to women.

First, the much more porous socio-spatial boundaries of the program deflected some of the potential pressures on women pursuing a traditionally male field in a predominantly male business school with a faculty heavily dominated by men. The principal forms of social organization and support were located *outside* the academic setting, in groups that were in some cases composed exclusively of women (e.g., the sororities). Women in management didn't have to depend on, let alone work with, the male students. Second, the relatively small number of courses requiring students to do group work on cases or solve problems may have been a factor: accounting, a very problem-oriented field where students did work together on homework problems in groups, *was* primarily male. Finally, management was nowhere near as time-consuming as physics. Women majoring in the field didn't have to devote the preponderance of their waking hours to it, nor did majoring in management commit one to further education or to a highly determined career path. The women majoring in management saw themselves in the future moving in and out of various jobs, perhaps changing careers altogether at some point. Melinda, for example, was about to take a personnel job upon graduation, but in the longer term she wanted to get married, have a family, and perhaps work programming computers out of her home: 'I want to work to live, not live to work'. While male management students expressed similar sentiments, such a statement would not have been made by a serious physics student of either gender.[7]

Unlike physics, then, where enrolment meant taking on the identity of 'physicist', a member of a scholarly community exploring how the world worked, a degree in 'management' wasn't attached, in student or faculty eyes, to a particular identity or ideology, or to the 'mastery' of a particular body of knowledge.

Courses That Do Not Constitute a Network

In physics, the temporal frame of academic activity was the entire sequence of physics courses leading to the Bachelor of Science degree. Faculty and students alike looked at the coursework as being substantively connected, either in the sense that later courses drew on practices introduced in the earlier ones, or in the sense that topics and issues were being cycled through in different courses at different levels of complexity. In management, by contrast, each course was essentially self-contained and separate from the courses that preceded or followed it. Unlike the time frame in physics that stretched across courses and years, the fifteen weeks of the semester was the relevant temporal unit in management: each course built up to a climax (usually a final test) and was then 'forgotten' as students began the next semester with different professors, students, and subject matter.

Where physics compressed social space inward toward the small problem-solving groups operating in the academic setting, and coiled time through the recursive treatment of topics, the management program expanded students' social space and fragmented their time into segregated, short-term episodes. By expanding social space I mean that the program extended the frame of student activity beyond the boundaries of the academic setting by connecting students to student organizations and business practitioners. By fragmenting time I mean the program created a temporal order composed of unconnected activities: the courses didn't build upon or relate to one another, and classwork consisted of brief, discrete tasks.

The most striking consequence of the short-term time frame was that students couldn't evaluate their courses in terms of their linkages to past or future academic experiences, and so weighed them directly in terms of what they considered the courses' 'everyday' or 'real-world' relevance. Students didn't question the general importance of accounting in business practice, for example, but they weren't sure of the relevance of the two required accounting courses to a management career: 'you know, if you're in business you usually have an accountant working for you' (Joe). 'Irrelevant' courses were either too 'theoretical', like Introductory Organizational Behaviour, which had students memorizing bits of organizational theory from Taylor through McGregor, or too specialized, like the Introductory Operations Management course, which required them to learn equations and do a lot of math problems. Students weren't the only ones who questioned the value of the quantitatively oriented 'management science' or 'operations management' courses. The adjunct faculty of the program, recently retired from the managerial world, flatly questioned their relevance, and one of the graduate students teaching the course conceded that:

> As a matter of fact, when they get out into the world, I'm not sure how much contact they'll have with the operations side of the business — at least in the United States the operations side has been neglected for a long time and everything was run by the finance people and the marketing people. So I really don't know how to answer that question — when they get in the real world, how much help will it be.[8]

In any event, *how* courses were taught seemed to make little difference to how students thought of them. Both marketing and finance were very large lecture courses: students were usually only required to take notes on the lectures, read the textbooks, and take multiple choice tests over the material. Yet marketing was disliked while finance wasn't. Marketing lacked 'practicality' (Joe) and according to Dorothy consisted mainly of 'numerous facts that I didn't think were particularly relevant to anything in life'. The finance courses drew more positive reactions from students because they were considered 'applicable' to everyday life. As Clara explained:

> [In the Managerial Finance class] you learn about investments, and you learn what is a good investment, how to determine if something is a good investment or a bad investment. You can really use that. It's real practical. I mean, it can be practical on a personal level, or at a corporate level.

Each course, then, was weighed for its relevance to the work world, an external space, rather than its relevance to other courses. If its relevance was weak the students judged the coursework harshly.[9] In the management program courses were presumed guilty until proven innocent. Delbert's comment illustrates the underlying suspicion:

> This'll probably sound bad, but I don't see how a lot of these classes are useful at all in the business world. I think the most useful thing is experience, internships, that type of thing. I mean, unless you're out there, you're not going to learn how businesses run through books and stuff. I mean, you get your basic ideas, but I know, one of my

friends got a job and they looked at him and said, 'anything you learned in the book, forget it, because we're going to teach you the way to do it our way' (Delbert).

Management students considered their coursework 'stilted', that is, 'more connected to theory, less connected to action' (Rhonda). The physics program avoided this problem — or rather, made a virtue of it — by creating a hermetic disciplinary space that produced disciplinary phenomena in the introductory courses and then mathematized them through a recursive curriculum. The program enrolled students in organizations of space and time where it was imperative to deal not with the physicality of the everyday 'subjective world', but with the phenomenal world constructed in the representational spaces of physics. And to get access to the phenomena of physics — the colliding particles, oscillating systems, and so forth that were constitutive of physics — one had to *do* physics (or learn to see everyday activity in physics terms).

In management, students were similarly pulled between two competing actor-networks trying to impose definitions on the phenomena of the business world: the program on one hand and on the other the business world itself, encountered through summer jobs, familial connections, and most importantly through the social networks they encountered in the business school. Unlike physics, however, the management program's interessements failed and the academic constructions of reality never approached those of the business world in importance for the students. For the moment I'll suggest that this lack of enrolment was a consequence of the fact that there was no obligatory course sequence in the program.

Students Shaping the Course Sequence

The spatial and temporal organization of academic work in the management program was shaped by student practice. Instead of having to fit their lives to the program's space-time regime, students could move in and out of the program with relative ease and fit its academic requirements into their ongoing patterns of activity. Physics students' time was monopolized by required courses that had to be taken in a strict sequence. Management majors took many more electives, and while some pairs of required courses were sequenced (e.g., the two accounting courses) there were no substantive links between them. As a result, management students didn't move through their courses together and the curriculum wasn't a site for forming friendships and crafting 'professional' identities. However, the fragmented course sequence did foster other forms of social organization that could impose a structure on the variable curricular landscape. I look first at how students mobilized information about courses and professors, then at how they inscribed and mobilized the courses themselves.

Because the content of management courses varied from professor to professor (even more so than in other business fields such as accounting), students' choices about when and from whom to take a class shaped the space-time organization of their coursework.

These choices were guided by student-organized advising networks instead of the official advising system run by the business school.[10] Some of this peer advising was informal: during registration, for example, when people congregated in the business building cafeteria to exchange information:

> In fact I had several people come up to me going 'What classes should I take?' And I'm going 'Well, you want an easy semester, do you want an average one, or a real hard one? Or do you want to learn a lot or not learn a thing?' (laughs). . . . And you get the general consensus that it's a tough class but you do learn something. And, ah, usually just people — you can walk around the business building the week before preregistration . . . and you're going 'Wait a minute, what's this person like?' And everybody's in the cafeteria and they're helping each other: 'You don't want this person!' (Sheena)

More often information on courses and faculty was managed by student organizations. According to Rhonda, students in the Management Organization group would tell her such things as 'This is a good course, this is a fun course, this teacher's really good, this is a course where you really have to work hard to make an A but it's very worthwhile. Things of that nature.' Sometimes meetings were arranged specifically to allow students to counsel each other:

> This next coming Tuesday, the Management Association is going to have a [meeting] about — we're just all going to get together and help each other out on who to take/who not to take. Or, 'if you want to take this, this is what you're going to have to do.' So people know what to expect. It makes you feel like — maybe it makes you feel like you have a jump on the next guy — and you probably do (Dell).

Fraternities and sororities (whose memberships were disproportionately composed of business majors) had institutionalized this process. Sheena explained:

> With the sororities and fraternities, what they do is like they put, like they put them all into alphabetical order. They put 'Money and Banking' and they'll put 'Dr X' beside it, and they'll have a list. They'll have a 'good list' and a 'bad list'. And the bad list are usually professors that are incoherent . . . or something is not kosher. And then you have to put your name under the stuff you wrote down. That means that people can come to you and ask you 'why didn't you like this class?' Like people will come to me and they're going to ask me 'well, Sheena, why didn't you like Managerial Finance with Dr Z?' And I'm going to go 'basically because of my attitude, I didn't care. I wanted a grade,

I wanted out of that class. I studied for it. I was just frustrated, because I tried and I couldn't do it. And therefore I don't like the class.' And they're going to go, 'oh, OK.' And I'll go, 'But, you know, if you're a finance major and you get into economics and accounting, then that's fine, you'll love the class. But for me, uh-uh.' . . . So it's what people want, it's not just good or bad.[11]

Instead of having their spatial and temporal trajectories shaped by program requirements, students organized the space-time relations among their courses. Schedules were composed for reasons unconnected with the substance of the courses. As Curtis explained:

I hate 8:00 classes. . . . And also I liked getting out early in the afternoon, which is OK. So I changed my 12:30 class to 9:30 so I could get out at noon, instead of having to break I have three straight classes. . . . I'd rather go twice a week for that than three times a week for 50 minutes — although three times a week goes by really quick as far as when you're in there. . . . And also, another thing I like is to be off on Fridays. I've done that on three semesters, I've been off on Fridays.

Instead of a curriculum producing a compressed, disciplinary social space, as in physics, management students shaped their curricular sequence to produce a minimal disruption to other social activites. This construction of the curriculum as an aggregation of unrelated courses, in conjunction with the temporal and spatial fragmentation that resulted from the course selection practices I've described, led management students to representational practices for mobilizing *coursework* rather than disciplinary phenomena.

Representational Production of Academic Space-Time

In the physics program note-taking, studying and problem-solving were parts of a cascade of representation that enmeshed students in the discipline's representational productions of space-time. Physical phenomena were reconstituted as stable, mobile and combinable forms that could be worked upon in physics practice. In the management program, by contrast, students inscribed or spatialized the social practice of their *classes* in movable forms that could be combined and consumed in a testing situation. These strategies of inscription varied from course to course. As Dorothy explained:

For a course such as the management class I'm taking right now, ah, he [the professor] emphasizes his lecture notes. I write down as much as I possibly can . . . partially because I do not want to miss anything, partially because it keeps me alert if I'm constantly writing . . . and I study the notes heavily because he strays from the book, he doesn't feel the book is complete. . . . As far as the book is concerned, I don't spend as much time on it as I would other classes, simply because he emphasizes notes.

Professors were the definers of relevance. Rather than performers demonstrating paths through a text-constituted space, management professors tried to use texts to formulate distant spaces (corporate settings and practices) that students were supposed to reproduce in movable forms (notes) and combine with textbook representations (written cases or theory summaries). What happened, however, was that students treated textbooks, lectures, and other tasks as representations not of the business world, but of the end of the semester, the test.

As far as I'm concerned, the first day, when they give you the syllabus and they lay out what they expect, that's probably the most valuable class. You know exactly what to do to get a certain grade. I don't always do it, but you know what you need to do. So I usually just go with the flow of the class; see how the class shapes up and what I need to do, try to lay it out like that (Dell).

I think intonation — just how teachers speak, you know what's important. I think basically if you just go into a class and listen, a teacher gives so many hints about what's important it's really easy to pick out. . . . Also I've gotten into the habit of, ah, if the teacher emphasizes that the book is very important; when I'm reading it I go through and outline everything. Ah, I think I'm a good listener in lectures. And I think I take good notes. I think I'm able to capture what the teacher's trying to say fairly well in my notes, and so it's basically just studying my notes and the book (Rhonda).

I take notes during class, whenever the teacher writes something on the board I put it down. Anything that he repeats I put down, or anything that seems important to me I'll put down. Or if he's a teacher that just follows the book strictly, I'll be flipping through the book and underlining what he has covered in the book, or putting a checkmark by it or circling that page number, scribbling a note in the margin (Dorinne).

Probably the luckiest attribute I have is that I'm able to pick out what the teacher says that is important. It may come from already having read the text. If the teacher's saying something that the textbook said, *that's* important. If the teacher is using an illustrative story, that's not as important to write down in detail. Ah, definitions are always important. Lists are always important. Charts and graphs are always important. Ah, it's quite simple if you've read the material and if you've paid attention to the syllabus and what the focus of the course is. If you've focused on that focus, then you should understand what to pick up (Melinda).

[You know what to concentrate on] mainly by what the instructor emphasizes. . . . Ever since I was a freshman, I've always believed that if a teacher wrote it down on the board, it was important enough for me to learn it. If it's something the instructor puts more force behind or spends maybe a lecture or a lecture and a half on, it's important. The textbook, if it's, ah, if it's — simple stuff, if it's bold face, if it's a title of a topic, or if it's continually repeated in the textbook, you keep being referred back to it (Jack).

In some cases professors gave fewer cues and students had to wait to see what kinds of material were being asked for on tests before knowing what portion of the textbook or the lecture to include in their notes:

Some teachers are just really difficult to take notes from — no type of structured lecture or anything. Just kind of off the wall. Like I've got a finance teacher now who just loves throwing quotes, and little stories out of *The Wall Street Journal*. I have no idea what to write down, so . . . in that class, I try to pick up on high points. He'll say something out of the book, and I'll make a note of like what he said and the page number. I try to follow him in the book. He goes pretty good about following the book. He just doesn't really elaborate much on it. And on the first two tests . . . what he's said out of the book is what's been on his tests, and not what he's drawn from *The Wall Street Journal*. So I don't even write those notes down. I just study what he says out of the book (Joe).

I take notes and I re-write my notes, and I also take notes from my readings, and then I combine the notes from the classes and readings, and that's what I study from — and hope that I picked out what they're going to test over. Most of the times I do. Sometimes I have no idea where they got the material for the test — it's not what I was studying (laughs) (Sonia).

Just as students compressed and mobilized the test-like aspects of their professors' performances in their notes, they distilled their textbooks to extract testable items in compressed forms. Unlike physics textbooks, which were tools and 'structuring resources' (Lave, 1988) for group study activity, management textbooks were consumable commodities. You couldn't get at the spaces and times of 'physics' outside texts of some kind, but management students came to the view that 'management' was necessarily *outside* the text. Textbooks were irrelevant to 'business reality'. In terms of academic practice, management students didn't have to move through a text-space or build space-time in text; they merely had to mobilize the texts in forms that could be combined and consumed (in short-term memorization) for one space-time event (the final test). Thus I'm less interested in the ideological assumptions in management texts (e.g., the depoliticized view of corporate life they present, see Pfeffer, 1981, p. 14) or in their accuracy (see Pethia, 1983) than in how students compressed them into more mobile forms.

Some students simply drew on their knowledge of tests as texts to transform ('edit') the books into test-preparation tools:

> As I read the book I highlight what I consider to be important and beginning from a week to two weeks before the exam, depending on how much material, I start going through and making outlines of the chapters in the book. Not as in Roman numeral one, a, b, c, d, as in, you know, just summaries. I feel that the knowledge, the material is put into my head better if I read it and write it down. . . .
> [*Nespor*: How do you know what to highlight in the book?]
> . . . I try to stay away from sentences that are blanket definitions. They stand out like a sore thumb, you can tell those. I rarely ever highlight those.
> [*Nespor*: Why not? I would think that's what's most likely to be on the test.]
> . . . Because in bold type it's obvious that it's important. So I don't take the time to underline it. Usually you can pick up a blanket definition, just on an exam, you know, it's obvious, 'number C is the blanket definition'. So if there are any blanket definitions those are pretty much obvious to me (Dorothy).

Other students tried to first compress the texts and then combine them with the classnotes:

> What I usually do, I get the book out and outline the chapters. Then I get the notes and kind of interrelate them with what I just outlined, and then just study like: I'd get a legal pad and outline a page a chapter, trying to put down all the good parts. And then with a different colour pen I'd put the notes in and stuff, and study like those for the next couple of days (Delbert).

In management all 'studying' — academic work in or out of the classroom — was focused on the tests (or in the classes that used them, the papers, case reports or game simulations that determined grades). While students differed in how they compressed textbooks into mobile formats (and some didn't read the books at all, accepting that this would hurt their grades but calculating that it wouldn't hurt them too much), all of the management students I interviewed used their mobilizations of the lectures and texts to compress the course spatially and temporally into as few pages that could be consumed in a short period (days or hours) just prior to the tests. 'Studying for the test' (a test being the ultimate compression of the course) meant replaying the course in a spatio-temporally compressed form:

> For a test . . . primarily I would study two or three days before the test. I felt like I could remember it better. So I'd go through, three days before a test, and maybe read all the chapters, go back, highlight chapters, and then from where I highlighted I would take notes. I figure if I write it down, I could see it on my paper and I could remember the material a lot better. I'd do that primarily for essay and multiple-choice tests (Joe).

> Everybody goes, you know, 'well, you should keep up with your reading, and all that stuff all the way through the semester'. Well, I did that on my first round of exams, and I got all Cs. And so I said 'blow this off'. And so my next . . . risk management insurance exam . . . was over six chapters. So the week before, I read all the chapters, and I outlined everything, and left it alone, and the night before I went over all the outlines: got a 96 on the exam. Cool, I've figured this one out. And so I did that for all my other exams and I got nothing below a 90. So I said, 'okay, now I've figured it out'. . . . I have to wait — that way it stays in my memory longer, and I can remember it. If I study something in January and I have to take an exam on it at the end of March, I'm not going to remember it (Sheena).

Like Sheena, most of the students had heard, and learned to ignore, the argument that 'good study skills' meant studying regularly throughout the semester rather than cramming. For most, cramming became standard practice:

> I *mainly* focus it before tests. . . . I'm not one of those good people that comes home from the lecture and reads over the lecture and learns it then. I've never been able to do that. That's not how I study. I study a lot before tests (Rhonda).

> You memorized it for the test and after the test was over you forgot what it was all about (laughs). . . . If it's a class I feel like I'm going to have difficulty in, I'll study them [my notes] every night. My management classes right now, I don't feel very threatened by them. I mean, I take the notes, and then I look at them the night after class — if I don't, fine — and then when test time rolls around I always start at least a week ahead for every test. And I spend one night getting organized, and then after a night of organization, then I go in and start spending two to two-and-a-half hours a night until the test. . . . Just reading them over. I rarely re-outline my notes or re-write them. The same way with textbooks, I don't outline the textbooks. I highlight, but I don't jot notes down. I don't outline textbooks (Jack).

This compression of time reached extreme proportions in some students' practices. They delayed studying to the last moment to force themselves to pick out the test-relevant material and ignore the rest:

> I try to read the material and then I go back through and just — the night before the test — I usually postpone it until I've got just a few hours to study, and I'm forcing myself to just skim and just hit the highpoints. And I can't afford to waste time with material that's not important. And somehow I just tend to prioritize it, without thinking about it.... I'll skim my notes.... In high school I never studied, period. But I did just fine. But in junior college I had to study a little bit more than in high school, but not much. But I found that if I crammed right before the exam I did about two letter grades better. Like I would make an A rather than a C... If I studied the way they tell you to study. I just couldn't seem to — maybe I learned the material better, maybe it stayed with me longer if I studied the right way, but if I want to make high grades, the best way to do it is to cram (Dorinne).

Even when such practices didn't produce high grades some students took pride in their ability to make adequate grades with a minimal expenditure of time. Curtis was the most hardcore crammer of this type:

> First of all, the notes of course, concentrate on them. You have to read the syllabus just a lot of times to get hints on things to stress. Or they'll give hints on whether the book's going to be more important or not more important.... I don't keep up with my reading on a regular basis like you should.... I'm a crammer.... Like I said, I think I know how to study real well. I really do. I'm good at picking up what's going to be in the test. I'm good at knowing what to study, because some of the cramming I've done in the past, normal people wouldn't be able to pass and I can pull Bs or Cs out of stuff that people wouldn't even be able to pass, period. For instance, not to be proud of this, but in my intermediate accounting, which is hard stuff, and I really didn't keep up in there because I'm taking it pass/fail, so for this first test — it was really pretty rough, and I studied the night before for about 10 hours, 10 or 12 hours, and I stayed up till 5:00 in the morning, got an hour's sleep... I read two chapters all the way through, kind of hard reading, kind of long, and I just flew over the homework, I didn't work it myself I just looked at the answers and figured out how they did it. Well, I ended up making like a C on the exam, but like I said, a lot of people with that type of thing wouldn't be able to. I mean, there's a lot of people who are keeping up, doing all the reading, doing the homework, and they still make Cs. And I can do it like the night or two before and make a C. So I think as far as

knowing what to study and how to study, I think I'm pretty good at that. . . . On that same thing, if I read the chapters and kept up and studied say, three hours every night, every night, then I could make a lot better grades, I could make As. And I don't make that many As because of my study habits, the way I do it. Although when I . . . stay up all night writing papers I usually do well in them (Curtis).

In physics the chapter-end problems were short journeys through physics space that allowed students to make sense of the expository sections of the textbooks. The test items were similar to the weekly homework problems except that the students had to work the former alone and within a limited time period. In both kinds of activities, students had to use the mathematical formalisms of the discipline to move through the text space. In management the problem was quite different. The students' task was to compress the space and time of a particular course (its lectures and its textbook(s)) into a form in which it could be, in a sense, consumed just prior to and then regurgitated in the test setting. Melinda, a straight-A student, described an extreme version of this process:

The most helpful thing I learned to do was to condense my notes. Because having to condense them means that you have to understand them. And I would condense it down to the smallest outline form and I could almost always reduce an entire chapter to a page. And so when it came to a final time, instead of being covered with this huge textbook over here and 20, 30, 40, 50 pages of notes over here — let's say the textbook had 12 chapters and the teacher had stayed with the textbook, I'd have 12 pages in front of me. Sometimes only the front of them. Because I would write real small, so it wouldn't be too much for me to handle, cause it looked like one piece of paper: 'I can do this'. It would all be on one piece of paper, so I could skim through it, and I would slam through, I would slam through those pieces of paper to the point where *I could go through the entire course in about 10 minutes before an exam!* That's what I would do before my finals. I'd just read my notes faster and faster and faster and condense them and condense them (Melinda).

'Understanding' the course meant being able to compress it spatially and temporally, to reconstruct it in a format that resembled the tests in their spatio-temporal parameters.

The Circulation of Academic Commodities

When I first started doing fieldwork I routinely asked students if they'd give me their notes after a course was over. I quickly realized I couldn't do much with the physics students' notes, that it was the process of taking them, trying to work ahead of the professor's lecture, that was important, not what was written down. In management, students had other uses for the notes and wouldn't give them to me. Melinda was the only management student I interviewed who destroyed hers: 'I just saw these mounds of paper that were too big for me to ever go back into, or to care to. You could never find anything in them.' A few students kept theirs, though usually for no particular reason (as Joe put it, 'I think I keep them just to have proof that I went to college'). Only Rhonda claimed to actually use old notes:

> My notes: I keep them in a file cabinet, and I usually do end up going back to them a lot for other classes. . . . There's one class where I'm working on — it's a marketing class and we have to go back and do a lot of financial analysis, and so I've gone back to my accounting notes and gone through some of that (Rhonda).

Most of the students in the program, by contrast, gave their notes to other students.[12] Notes, tests, and papers done for a class were routinely circulated to students about to take the class. As one student explained:

> I save all [my notes], I have them all up on a shelf. Some people I know, younger, I've given them to, and I've gotten a lot of notes from people. . . . You might have an old test or two and you can see how they're doing it. It helps a lot to study off of those. That's been a big difference this semester, too. Every single class that I've had was re-commended to me. I think that's made a big difference, no question (Dell).

> A lot of times, I'll take all of my notes, plus I'll copy someone else's — not a lot, I've done this with two courses — and copy someone else's notes to supplement mine, to get both of our's perspectives (Clara).

Notes were passed down across generations of students:

> A lot of people, . . . they come up and ask 'did you have such and such a class?' 'Yeah'. 'What were the tests like?' 'Well here's my test, my old test, my old notes and stuff.' I mean, I got all these notes from other people, they just keep getting passed down the line. So, I mean, I have them all, and I had a lot of them I've given away. So they've come in helpful, like me using other people's notes, cause I mean, it's the same class, but they'll get stuff out of it, maybe, that I wouldn't have . . . that's been really useful. It's just another set of notes that I would coincide with my notes, which I would then coincide with the outline of the chapters to try to get the basic ideas, the main points of the course (Delbert).

Tests and writing projects (term papers) were also circulated:

> I save them all. . . . I save tests — I try to save as many tests as I can. And I put them in the Phi Chi Theta test file, for other people, to help them. . . . In fact I'm bringing some calculus tests today (Clara).

These test files were not secret. In addition to the ones controlled by student organizations like Clara's, professors of quantitatively oriented courses such as finance usually put sample tests on file in the university library — and students knew of at least one course with tests on file that were still being used. Papers, on the other hand, were circulated only through student organizations. Bart, a senior, described the practice of writing projects:

> being passed on and somewhat amended in different areas to change it a little bit. So you've got a 20 page project that's due for professor X, and you've got a friend that says 'hey, I had professor X, I did this project, let me give it to you.' I think there's a lot of that going on. . . . Either that, or modelling it after another. Which would save a lot of time (Bart).

Sonia, a commuting student who didn't belong to any student organizations, told me that:

> [Students] that are in a fraternity or sorority — if they have to write a paper they have tons on file they can choose from, and just kind of re-write it a little bit. I mean, I've had several tell me that's what they do. . . . And they make real good grades, but I don't think they learn anything (Sonia).

Neither Bart nor Sonia was especially upset by this practice (although they said they didn't indulge themselves), and both seemed to think that the professors were aware of it — Sonia suggested it was one reason so few papers were assigned in business courses. In terms of my argument, this circulation of coursework reflected a spatial compression of academic activity that allowed students to organize the curriculum in a representational space-time — e.g., laying out syllabuses and course assignments on tables and examining various possible configurations — just as they organized the material space-time of the program through their course-taking decisions. These activities, once again, did not mobilize distant business-world phenomena, or create a phenomenal world in a representational space, or even help students to become facile with the discipline's representational technologies. Instead, they led to the crafting of commodities that had only local exchange value (exchange for a grade, exchange in the student social networks). How was this separation of the management program from the business world accomplished?

Separating Worlds

We can examine how the 'irrelevance' of the management courses was constructed by looking at the last management course students took: Managerial Strategy. Faculty called this the program's 'integrative course' because it was supposed to force students to use what they'd learned in previous classes, especially accounting, finance and marketing,[13] in coursework 'relevant' to real business practice. Of course, given the study practices I've described it should be no surprise that students couldn't draw on their previous coursework and recounted experiences similar to Melinda's. As a straight-A student she was:

> very surprised to learn what I hadn't remembered. I go through all these classes . . . but you ask me what I learned in my Accounting, Financial Accounting, I don't know. I really don't know. I passed the test and I forgot. . . . I guess business is just something you have to work with every day to keep sharp on it. But I had to sit down the other day and really learn what I learned in Financial Accounting, surface, I had to learn beneath it.

Managerial Strategy faculty accommodated students by briefly reviewing the needed subject matter from previous courses (which was, in any case, minimal), and moved on to the two main components of the course: case analyses (some done individually, some done by teams of two or three students) and the 'Business Game' — a computer simulation in which the students, split into teams, competed against each other running firms in an imaginary economy.[14]

The Business Game

The Business Game or 'B-game', as it was known to students, was a computer simulation of manufacturing firms (teams of three or four students) 'competing' with each other in the single market.[15] Students chose their own teams, but rarely knew other people in the class and thus often worked with strangers. Each team began with the same assets and had to make weekly decisions about how many items to produce, how many machines to buy, which regions to expand into, how much to pay salesmen, how much to borrow, and so forth. These 'decisions' were entered into a computer where a program determined how many items the teams would sell, what their profits would be, and so forth. Teams were ranked at the end of each week (on the basis of profit and return on investment) and grades were awarded on the basis of the group's final ranking. According to one of the designers of the simulation:

> The basic goal of the game is to reward careful creative planning and it develops a skill in analyzing what is happening and then reacting

to the competition and other factors that are either favourable or unfavourable to the partners and the firm.

In the terms I've been using, the goals of the designers were very ambitious: they wanted to produce versions of disciplinary social spaces — teams in competition for real rewards (grades) — and they wanted the groups to employ disciplinary representations of space (plans, etc.). In practice, however, the students' 'strategy' and 'planning' were not directly assessed. The professors embraced an imagined, representational space of 'the market' in which the groups' 'monetary' outcomes could be treated as veridical evidence for the quality of their stategies:

> We follow the principle that the quality of strategy and the quality of their implementation is reflected in two things: the total net profit earned and the way they deal with the assets under their control. They have the opportunity to shrink them or expand them, and so we grade them on two things: the net profit earned and the return on total investments. And we measure them and they are then ranked from one to ten.

As the students interpreted this, it was the end result rather than the logic and depth of their planning that counted:

> I mean, that's the whole goal, that's all they care about over there, is we have to make money. I'm in a class right now where 30 per cent of my grade depends on how much money I make in this imaginary company. That's the whole thing. They don't care how I do it, just so I make money. And that is the emphasis in the business school (Melinda).

The game's emphasis on short-term profit maximization rather than strategic planning was widely known in student lore. When I interviewed Dorothy before she'd taken the course, she talked of having:

> heard some horror stories about people who have really approached it rationally, trying to be an ongoing concern, and make big expenditures now that will pay off in the future — and this class only lasts three months and there's really no future, and they end up consistently being the lowest ranked group. And have gotten quite a lot of anxiety out of that. So . . . I have a feeling I'm going to keep that in the back of my mind: make money, make money, make money [in the short-term].

In some ways this short-term orientation may not have been unreasonable. Harvey (1989), for example, points out that the space-time compression of national and international economies:

makes it extremely difficult to engage in any long-term planning. . . .
This means either being highly adaptable and fast-moving in response
to market shifts, or masterminding the volatility. The first strategy points
mainly towards short-term rather than long-term planning, and culti-
vating the art of short-term gains wherever they are to be had. This
has been a notorious feature of US management in recent times (pp.
286–7).

The problem with the game, though, was that in addition to the short-
term orientation it had a lot of features that made it seem unrealistic to students. Bart pointed out that the tactics and strategies allowed by the game
were severely limited:

> you don't have lead time, you can make contract purchases and single
> order purchases, and, yeah, you save money by contract purchases, but
> that's almost obvious, I think. So areas need a little bit more intricacy,
> to be able to take more input from you.

Jack, who had worked for manufacturing firms in summer jobs, pointed
out that the game decontextualized the social nature of business practice:

> the B-game is fairly random, mainly because you don't have a whole
> lot of information. It's actually kind of vague, considering — like
> entering markets and stuff like that, that you know nothing about. It's
> highly unlikely for a business, you wouldn't enter the market if you
> knew zero about it, zero about the price and about your competi-
> tion. . . . Here in school it's all done on paper. You don't see the items
> come in, you don't see the items going out, you don't understand the
> severity of a back order, because on the job you have a customer
> screaming down your neck asking you where the product is, and in
> school it's just, 'well, you have a back order. That's cost you $10 this
> quarter.' That's it. So it's a big difference, because [in the real world]
> you're dealing with the public and you're dealing with the items them-
> selves instead of just watching the items flow on paper.

Of course, as the physics case demonstrated, the fact that a pedagogical
activity doesn't resemble disciplinary practice doesn't mean it can't serve to
enrol students in the disciplinary actor-network. And as Jack's comments suggest, the business game paralleled in interesting ways the homework problems
of the physics program: the group work (here compulsory rather than student-
initiated), the weekly cycle, the completely textualized interaction with the
subject matter. Indeed, the creation and use of the game probably reflected an
attempt to make management and management education more 'scientific' in

some sense. The problem was that students' trajectories through material spaces had already acquainted them with business practice: they were all, in a sense, in the position of the physics student Paul who'd worked in a lab and hence saw academic problems as 'completely orthogonal to real life situations'.

Instead of 'rational planning' — the legitimate way of temporalizing business activity from the perspective of the professors — students dealt with the game by making ad hoc, situation to situation decisions. Velma, for example, gave this account of how she went about making decisions:

> As far as analyzing ratios and that kind of thing, I didn't do it, I kind of work with my gut instinct: 'let's try this, I think it'll work' or 'it looks like the price is what's going to make the difference here, this quarter, based on last quarter.' And then it turned out through experience [in the b-game] that it was how much you paid your salesmen that was going to benefit. So it was just kind of a gut instinct. We had a strategic plan, but we didn't really stick with it all the way.

Sheena was even more blunt:

> We had no idea what we were doing the entire time. We came in 4th [out of 10] (laughs). Had no idea at all. Someone said 'watch inventories', so we said 'okay', so we watched for it. We had no idea at all . . . we had fun doing it. It was kind of 'well, let's try this'. And I think that the main thing that was kind of frustrating was that there was no way to get your salesmen to sell more, without — 'cause they would say [the computer would send a message], 'okay, we want an increased salary' — you'd get a little notice 'salesman #13 will quit if you don't raise his salary by $100 or $200' or whatever. So we'd raise it. We ended up paying these dudes $2,000 a piece. And they had like 80 per cent commissions, and they had expense accounts that wouldn't quit. And we'd raise their commissions and they'd still want more salary. 'No'. So that ate our lunch as far as our fixed costs. I learned a lot that way, I said like 'can't we have little promotional deals, give little bonuses or awards or something?' But the computer program says it's not possible.

Such experiences led students to conclude that the game was meant to teach them how difficult and unpleasant it was to work with other people (to a person, management students disliked working in groups), to teach them the randomness of the business world, to teach them that there would be situations where they'd have to make decisions without the necessary information, and to teach them that their superiors (in this case the professors, who were pointedly unhelpful in explaining the game) would rarely offer direction or take responsibility for a decision (cf. Jackall, 1988).

Case Analyses

In addition to the simulation, the Managerial Strategy course required students to do a number of analyses of business 'cases'. The case is a nationally-distributed representational technology that had its origins, according to Orth (1963), at the Harvard Business School, where it's 'the basic pedagogical technique employed in all of the educational programs' (pp. 32–3). According to the Harvard Business School Catalog:

> In the business world, where every decision must be appropriate to the specific situation and no two situations are identical, it is the ability to analyze, to judge trends, to weigh diverse influences, that leads to sound judgment; and that ability can be developed only through practice.
>
> Therefore, from the outset the students at the Business School discuss cases, i.e., real business situations in which executives take action and are responsible for the results. . . .
>
> The students study the case individually. Then they meet in small groups for further exploration, sharing their varied backgrounds of experience and sharpening their ideas in argument (quoted in Orth, 1963, p. 33).

The case was the most pervasive pedagogical format in management education, and variants of it could be found in most management textbooks: in the introductory texts 'cases' might be no more than brief vignettes, but by Managerial Strategy — the final course in the curriculum — they were full-blown, running 20–30 pages, accounting for the vast majority of textbook pages, and structuring the majority of students' course activity. They followed a typical formula: the depiction of a particular firm (usually a real enterprise like Mary Kay Cosmetics or Coors Brewing), described in a certain vocabulary of finance and management, as at a 'decision point' in the history of its operation. In analyzing the case students were usually expected to assume the role of 'managers': weighing the information provided and making a 'decision' about the firm's future. In theory what's important is not just *which* decision students make, but how they justify and explain their decisions.

Consider the case as a technology for mobilizing the world. Corporate 'management' was not enacted in the material spaces of the business school. Instead, it was mobilized in the contents of textbooks, lectures, and so forth that flowed through the space-time of the program along with the students. The particular substance of the mobilizations — the firms and decision issues that the cases are about — are less important than their form and function, which presumes a 'rational' decision-maker with access to all available information selecting a well-defined decision option in a depoliticized setting. Harvard exported this technology for constructing the substance of business education (although there are now even bigger secondary distribution points), and simultaneously (that is, by the same action) established it as an 'obligatory passage point' in the the network of representational accumulation (if you want to describe business practice for business education, you must use the format and conventions of the case).

What was being mobilized in the case method? It was not the professors' ideals of 'rational decision-making' (cf. Orth, 1963). At the school I studied students viewed the cases as short-term tasks to be done for a grade, with only the thinnest of connections to the 'real world' of business. Although the cases used in the strategic management course were descriptions of events in the lives of real corporations, they were temporally and spatially dislodged from the world of business. Students read them as incomplete accounts of past history:

> Well, to be honest with you I don't really know [what the point of the case analysis is]. I think it might be a little bit more beneficial if we could read the case, solve it ourselves, and see how it was actually solved, and whether that solution worked or not. But as far as just solving the case on our own; we don't get any input as far as what actually happened in the case. We could be shooting in the dark all the time (Jack).

As Bart explained: 'We're using old cases, but they tell you not to look at what's happened since then.' In spite of the authentic nature of the material (the cases often incorporated documents and data produced in corporate practice), the cases moved the business activity they described out of corporate space-time — in which problematic situations have to be resolved and consequences follow from the decisions of managers — into the frame of academic work, where a multitude of decisions were allowable (if students could make a good case for them) and the only consequences that followed were the grading and evaluation decisions of the professor. Rather than situating students in the social space-time of business the cases distanced students from it. As a result, students treated each case as a distinct event. They didn't use what they had applied in one case analysis to analyses of later cases — at least not the way the professors probably wanted them to: Curtis boasted of re-using the same graph and chart, unrevised, in different case analyses, having guessed that the grader was focusing on the quality of the graphic work rather than its substance or relevance to the case at hand:

> *Curtis:*   Listen to this one. I used — I showed Delbert — the same, where's my old case — [shows Dorothy his Walt Disney case] — Look at this [shows her an elaborate graph] Walt Disney — I got a 'good' on it, I even got a 'good' on it!
> *Dorothy:*   What'd you do the graph on?
> *Curtis:*   Look, Mary Kay [shows her same graph].

> *Delbert:*   Same graph! [general laughter].
> *Curtis:*   A photocopy.

One way of discussing these kinds of accounts would be to suggest that the program achieved the irrelevance of its courses by transforming academic knowledge into a kind of commodity, spatially and temporally segregated from everyday practice, exchangable for grades (Kvale, 1983, p. 445). In such situations we could speak of academic knowledge being mystified. Grades and knowledge would 'appear as independent beings endowed with life, and entering into relation . . . with one another' (Marx, 1967, p. 72; see Nespor, 1990c, for a different perspective on the grade economy in undergraduate education). Lave and Wenger (1991) evoke this line in suggesting that:

> where there is no cultural identity encompassing the activity in which newcomers participate and no field of mature practice for what is being learned, exchange value replaces the use value of increasing participation. The commoditization of learning engenders a funda-mental contradiction between the use and exchange values of the outcome of learning, which manifests itself in conflicts between learn-ing to know and learning to display knowledge for evaluation (p. 112).

One of the problems with this analysis, however, is that 'making deci-sions' for their short-term exchange value may well reflect the practices of 'full participants' in the managerial community (i.e., the distinction between 'ex-change' and 'use' value may not hold for 'political labour' (Collins, 1979) as opposed to productive labour). For example, Jackall (1988) gives this quote from an 'upper–middle level' manager as a representative statement on the nature of corporate decision-making:

> There's a tremendous emphasis put on decision-making here and in business in general. But decision-making is not an individual process. We have training programs to teach people how to manage, we have courses, and all the guys know the rhetoric and they know they have to repeat it. But all these things have no relationship to the way they actually manage or make decisions. The basic principles of decision-making in this organization and probably any organization are: (1) avoid making any decision if at all possible; (2) if a decision has to be made, involve as many people as you can so that, if things go south, you're able to point in as many directions as possible (p. 78).

Management students may have approximated 'legitimate practice' when they subverted the stated function of the case method and opted for short-term reward and the use of 'rationality' as rhetoric rather than the cultivation of 'rationality' as practice. Indeed, rationality as practice may exist only in academic representations of space, fulfilling a kind of allegoric function in the management students' educations.

The Case as Allegory

'Allegories', as Smadar Lavie (1990) puts it, 'are texts telling an individual story to convey a lesson for the whole group', a private story that attempts to represent the collectivity as a whole' (p. 29). The 'case' is allegorical in just this sense: not that the particular business situation described is supposed to represent that of all firms, but that the processes and circumstances of 'rational' decision-making it formulates are defined as central elements of the practices of managers considered as a collectivity. But Lavie also goes on to quote Greenblat's (1981) argument that:

> Allegory arises in periods of loss, periods in which a once powerful theological, political or familiar authority is threatened with efface-ment. Allegory arises, then, from the painful absence of that which it claims to recover, and, . . . as the paradox of an order built upon its own undoing cannot be restricted to this one discursive mode, in-deed, . . . the longing for an origin whose loss is the necessary condi-tion of that longing is the character not only of all discourse but of human existence itself (p. xviii, quoted in Lavie, 1990, p. 30).

The business 'case', I think, is best understood as an allegory of a 'tech-nical' or 'instrumental' rationality celebrated by experts and bemoaned by the academic left, but in practice a representation of space accomplished not by corporate officers managing companies but in the practices of academics and analysts. If the program had been part of a trajectory leading students into academia (and if the social space of academic management studies were con-tiguous with the spaces of corporate practice), the cases, like the textual forms in physics, might have functioned as spaces on the page (mobilizations of distant practices). But management students were on a trajectory out of aca-demia. There was a divide between the academic program and business spaces, and case analyses were thus more like public performances of 'rational' decision-making that, in good allegorical fashion, established for students the absence of that rationality. The case was a space-in-the-page, an imagined or represen-tational space that could not be produced outside the social space of the academic program. Students used case texts as parts of ritualized performances instead of working on them to become producers of a disciplinary representa-tional space (as did their peers in the physics program).

In the end, then, I don't think it'd be appropriate to say that students described the management courses as irrelevant *because of* internal peda-gogical characteristics or a lack of connection to real-world business practices (if this were how things worked surely physics students would have found their coursework far more irrelevant). Irrelevance was not an inherent feature of the courses but the outcome of a struggle between the school and the work world: the consequence of the school's failure to enrol students in an academic network.

But, again, it won't work to just say that the program didn't enrol students in the academic discipline. There are always multiple actor-networks vying to enrol people and things, and the fact that students coming *to* the program along such diverse trajectories could leave it with such similar accounts of their experiences suggests that there had to be another, more powerful actor-network working *within the business school context*, creating interessements separating students from the academic portion of the curriculum. Where I could tell a story about the physics program as enrolment into a powerful network, there are two stories to tell about management: the one just finished of the failed enrolment of students into an academic network, and the one to come, of their enrolment and bodily mobilization in business.

Notes

1   The department chair's comments also reflect a particular kind of rhetoric common among businessmen and business educators since at least the late 1950s: a valuation of broad training and a rejection of specialization and vocationalism (Gordon and Howell, 1959; Pierson *et al.*, 1959).

   However, as Gordon and Howell (1959, p. 117) pointed out long ago, there is a 'certain schizophrenic tendency' in the corporate attitude: a stated desire for liberal arts preparation, but recruiting practices that emphasize specialized vocational preparation in business. In part, as Jones (1986, p. 129) suggests, this reflects the specialization of the hiring function and its decoupling from the decision-making domains of top executives.

2   Adjunct faculty could be quite critical of the rest of the department, though few 'tensions' arose because the adjuncts were essentially isolated and ignored by the regular faculty (cf. Nyre and Reilly, 1979). One retired CEO of a middle-sized regional corporation, whose elective course on management trends was very popular among students, complained that 'the students were the forgotten customers. I think these bastards [the regular faculty] chase around and play politics with each other.' Another adjunct faculty member commented that much of the emphasis in the department seemed to him irrelevant on the basis of his 36 years as a manager with a multinational corporation.

3   It should be emphasized that these descriptions of field structuration refer to the *undergraduate programs* in physics and management, not to the fields themselves (for the latter see, e.g., Whitley, 1984).

4   The tight coupling between university and high school coursework found in physics was absent in business. High school business courses were not connected to undergraduate programs of study. Students who'd taken high school business courses and expected college business courses to be a continuation of them were quickly disillusioned.

5   There was, in fact, a kind of cascade of programs that students descended as they were pushed out of demanding programs: while business got many of those who

left engineering and the sciences, the liberal arts got many of the students who left business. Thirty-seven per cent of all students graduating with sociology degrees over a one-year period were former business students who'd flunked out of the program (from a transcript analysis).

6   A notable difference between the two fields was the level of 'occupational inheritance'. None of the physics students had parents who were physicists, but several of the business students were consciously choosing to follow their parents into business — although in every case the students had initially tried majoring in a non-business field. The inheritance of business occupations is apparently relatively common. Werts (1973), using surveys of freshmen in the early 1960s, found a strong 'father-choice' model guiding students' decisions to major in business: 44 per cent of all males choosing business as a major were sons of business men (1 per cent was the figure for physics) (there were no parallel calculations for women, apparently because so few women chose either field at the time). Hurtado (1989) also found a strong 'inheritance' of business as a career field (about 28 per cent among freshmen of both sexes). Three of the students I interviewed fell into this pattern.

7   Hearn and Olzak (1981) argue that men are more likely than women to choose undergraduate programs tightly coupled to specific occupations in fields offering high status rewards. Such programs 'emphasize training, discipline, and technical skills rather than the general intellectual, moral or social growth of students.' Women, supposedly, 'emphasize internal, instrinsic, immediate rewards over external, extrinsic, deferred rewards in choosing their majors' (p. 197). Hearn and Olzak (1981) conclude that 'men tend to opt for unsupportive departments conferring higher rewards, while women tend to opt for supportive departments with lower rewards' (p. 202). Eisenhart's (1985) study of women's career choice decisions lends partial support to these conclusions, though she emphasizes that women do consider extrinsic rewards such as monetary return in their career choices — they merely appear to give such factors less weight than men. Although it's a less discipline-oriented and 'high status' field than physics, it's hard to see what 'internal, intrinsic, immediate rewards' management could offer to females or males.

8   These arguments echo debate among analysts of undergraduate business education:

> Among the many entering the business world, fewer come prepared with the necessary levels of communication skills, cognitive abilities, and human understandings that are requisite for success beyond the entry level. The technical bent of business study can equip students with narrow problem-solving approaches destined for an early obsolescence. The underlying rationale of business study at many colleges is also flawed: it assumes that business 'is populated by rational executives who operate in a systematic results-oriented fashion.' Of course, those who have spent 'even a brief time in the business world know that this is rarely true (Mandt, 1982, p. 49). . . . 'Number crunching' is the thing to do, and students attack the 'multidimensional, consequential problems of enterprise with largely unidimensional, inconsequential mathematical models and similarly limited paradigms of human behaviour' (Behrman and Levin, 1984, p. 141) (Jones, 1986, p. 134).

9   Though no more so, I should point out, than corporate managers. Useem (1986) points out that over 80 per cent of managers (regardless of college major) report that their managerial skills were learned on the job (p. 86). The skills that corporate officers listed as most important for managers — most of them dealing with communicative and interactional skills — were not among those emphasized in the program's academic work:

For the internal labour market of the corporation, then, the specific content of college learning typically plays little role in the manager's performance or advancement (Useem, 1986, p. 87).

A collegiate specialization in business does seem to be related to obtaining an entry-level position (Useem, 1986, p. 87), but Useem argues that this is less because of any genuine connection between the courses and managerial competencies, than because the business major and business course-taking are taken as tokens of business motivation by recruiters:

As perceived by employers, liberal arts students attending an institution without a business concentration had no choice but to major in the liberal arts, while liberal arts students at a college with a business major could have chosen it but opted not to do so. The latter are riskier hires than the former, company recruiters infer, since the latter appear to have rejected business values (Useem, 1986, p. 88).

10 All but three of the interviewed students availed themselves of these kinds of advising networks (two of the three exceptions had outside jobs, and selected courses on the basis of what would fit into their schedules, the third 'researched' courses by sitting in on the first class session, looking over the syllabus and the teacher, and then adding courses late). Every management student I talked to said the official advising system was hard to use: it was centralized for the entire business school rather than departmental-specific, meaning students had to wait for long periods of time to see advisers who were mostly kept busy by seniors wanting them to check graduation requirements. Once students got to an adviser they found them unfriendly and their advice unreliable.

11 This was not always a sure-fire method, as students had to pre-register for their courses and the instructors listed in the catalog were often not the ones who actually taught the courses. Clara, for example, had heard that a particular statistics instructor was good, 'So I signed up for the class — but she's not teaching it anymore and I have a Chinese person (laughs). So it doesn't always work.'

12 With the growth of independent note-taking services at many large universities (for-profit companies that send note-takers to classes and then market the notes to students) this circulation of notes across student networks may change. Only one of the students I interviewed, Clara, talked of having relied on bought notes (she got a B in the course).

13 'Integrative', senior-level courses in 'business policy' were promoted in foundation reports of the late 1950s (see Gordon and Howell, 1959, pp. 206–7).

14 Unlike the physics students, management students did not usually work in groups, and found in the group work required for Managerial Strategy an endless source of complaint. Sometimes they complained of the difficulty of coordinating meetings outside class and getting the work done on time, but more often the problem was getting people to do their fair share of work:

There wasn't any structured way of organizing it. . . . And it turned out, me and the guy I knew were the only ones who did the work, the other two really didn't care, they were graduating in August and just said, 'let them do the work, we'll take the credit for it.' . . . There was enough work for four people, and we were doing it with only two. It wasn't a good situation. . . . [The professor] said, that was our responsibility to take care of it — which, you know, we tried, but it didn't really work (Joe).

An underlying reason group activity didn't work well was that students didn't move through the courses together and thus often didn't know or had never worked before with the people with whom they ended up being grouped.

15   Simulations similar in aim and design to the B-game began appearing in business school curricula in the 1950s (probably inspired by simulation programs used in corporate training) and became widely used after receiving strong endorsements from some of the national studies of undergraduate business training in the late 1950s (see Gordon and Howell, 1959, pp. 367–8).

Chapter 5

Mobilizing Bodies for Management

Those who run the bureaucratic corporation often rely on outward manifestations to determine who is the 'right sort of person'. Managers tend to carefully guard power and privilege for those who fit in, for those they see as 'their kind' (Kanter, 1977, p. 48).

Bodies, then, are not born; they are made (Haraway, 1991, p. 208).

Unlike physics, the 'cascade of representation' in the management program didn't involve the representation of inanimate phenomena in increasingly 'abstract' (that is, stable, mobile and combinable) forms.[1] True, academic course work was 'textualized' or reduced to stable and mobile written forms (notes) that could be combined and consumed in the semester climax (the final) and then circulated among other students. However, there were no pathways connecting that work to networks of managerial practice (although both educational and professional settings shared an instrumental, short-term orientation). Physics students were expected to continue to graduate school: the disciplinary ideology was spatially compressing, bringing the physical world under control by reducing it and constituting it in mathematized terms. For management students, association with the academic discipline ended on graduation, by which time students had come to accept a sharp division separating academic and business worlds.

There were, none the less, key pathways that connected the management program to corporate space. To see them we have to look at the organization of material spaces and bodily practices: at the production of mimetic environments and the strategic construction of bodies. For instead of compressing students' spatial arenas and putting them on a pathway leading to settings of disciplinary practice, as in physics, the management program routed students into a zone organized as an analog of corporate space. Instead of physics' mobilization of the world through textualizing space, the representational organization of space-time in management connected the program to the work world by mobilizing social practice in an *embodied* form.

Mimicry of Corporate Space

Plush carpets, potted trees, burnished oak wall panelling, fine reproductions and sometimes originals of great art, mahogany desks, polished

110

glass tables and ornaments, rich leather upholstery, perfectly coiffured, attractive and poised receptionists, and private, subsidized cafeterias are only a few of the pleasant features that grace the corporate headquarters of any major corporation (Jackall, 1988, p. 36).

Physics students were routed into progressively smaller spaces and tighter temporal regimes that cut them off from alternative *academic* actor-networks (other programs of study). Management students, by contrast, reserved substantial amounts of time for non-academic activity, and spent most of their time on campus in the business building, a material organization of space that, instead of cutting business students off from other academic programs (several had double majors) reinforced the divide between 'academic' and 'non-academic' worlds and contributed to the devaluation of the academic world.

The business building reinforced the academic-non-academic divide by producing a public space that mimicked the spatial form of the corporate workplace. The coursework may have been typical lecture and test, but the material settings of practice — and ultimately the social spaces they produced — were tied to those of the corporation both metaphorically (through simulations of corporate furnishings) and metonymically (though visible invocations of corporate links).

The business school building was a huge, labyrinthine structure housing a complex system of hallways connecting classrooms, offices, study lounges, computer workrooms, dining halls and courtyards. All business classes were conducted there (or in a newer business building connected to it by an above-ground walkway). Unlike the austere physics building, the business school wasn't geared solely to academic or scholarly activity. The wide landings, lobbies and hallways of the building, all lined with deep cushioned couches, were sites where students chatted between classes, read the newspaper, and waited for each other. This public interior space was organized in large part to simulate corporate space and function as a stage for the display of sociability. The large, open entranceways to the building advertised the corporate ties of the school. Their walls were covered with large plaques bearing the names of major donors who had funded chairs or professorships, while smaller plates bore the logos and names of other corporate and individual sponsors. The furnishings and artwork in the building (unlabelled original paintings in Minimalist or Colorfield styles, Oldenburg-like sculptures)[2] reflected corporate tastes in interior decoration, and the large hallways served as social spaces for displays of business demeanour and dress.

In management and business generally, students and faculty occupied physically distinct and socially distanced spaces. The academic faculty had a wing of the building to themselves for departmental and private offices and there were elaborate arrangements to restrict and regulate student movement through this area. Each department occupied a separate floor with a central, glass-enclosed secretarial suite ringed by faculty offices. A notice on the doorway leading to the faculty offices instructed visitors and students to check in with the secretaries before entering. Most office doors had plaques identifying the occupant and many had notices of office hours taped to them. Faculty and students were visible to one another but their spaces were never intermingled. Faculty resided in closed, symbolically restricted areas into which students, if they were permitted at all, went in and out.[3]

A good example of this separation was the organization of eating in the building. The business school had its own cafeteria system (the only other school with a cafeteria was Fine Arts, which was located on the periphery of the campus). Once, before a remodelling of the complex, faculty and students had shared a single dining hall (as was the case in Fine Arts). Now, they ate in two separate areas. For students there were short serving lines offering inexpensive fast-food breakfasts and lunches that could be eaten at long rectangular tables in the large, well-lighted dining hall. Next to the dining hall, separated from it by a wall of glass, was a three-story commons topped by an opaque-glass skylight. Boxed plants gave the area an informal feeling and there were benches for sitting and eating and space for student organizations to set up tables. Across this commons, enclosed by another wall of glass, was the faculty dining hall. Sitting in their dining hall or the commons students could look across and see faculty and their lunch guests sitting at the small round clothed tables, the food barely visible in a buffet-style serving area. When privacy was desired, the faculty dining room could be hidden from student view by drapes.

In addition to the separate spaces they controlled, faculty and students shared spaces. The most important of these were the interviewing areas and the advising office, both spaces in which students enacted their subordinate statuses within the program.

The business school had the most elaborate placement office on campus, taking up a floor of one wing of the building. In one set of offices, counsellors helped students write résumés, find out more about the corporations by whom they were about to be interviewed, and prepare for their interviews. Outside these offices there was a wall covered with a bulletin board where sheets were posted listing the corporations that would be interviewing on campus, the kinds of positions they were trying to fill, and the dates of the interviews. Students would cluster around these lists looking for jobs that interested them, and signing up to request interviews. The placement office scheduled the interviews, either on first-come first-serve basis or, if the corporation requested, sorting through the interested students and weeding out those whose grade point averages were too low.

The interviews themselves took place in a corridor lined with church pew-like benches built into the walls. Young men in dark suits (kept buttoned) with conservative ties, and women dressed in dark skirted suits, white blouses, and scout scarves, waited nervously for an interviewer to step out, shake their hand, and ask them into the room. The rooms themselves were small and bare: a table, chairs, some small reproductions of photographs or art on the white walls.

The administrative and advising offices were also subordinating spaces. To see one of the several undergraduate advisers you had first to enter a glass-enclosed lobby, wait in line at one of three windows to make an appointment, take a seat on one of the always crowded benches along the walls and wait for your name to be called, then be let through a door into the back area where the advisers had their offices.[4] I went through the process myself trying to set up an interview with a counsellor and felt as though I was at a dentist's office.

In these subordinating spaces students waited. In the placement area they waited for interviews, brief but intense encounters with corporate recruiters. In the advising area they waited for review and evaluation of their transcripts, for advisers to certify that they'd been taking the right courses and keeping their grade averages high enough to permit their continued enrolment in the program.

In classrooms, by contrast, students listened, looked, wrote, and, on occasion, spoke. Classrooms were not so much subordinating spaces as a no-man's land in which both students and faculty were transitory inhabitants. The business school contained several mammoth lecture halls seating hundreds of students in terraced semi-circles of thin tables and seats sloping down to the lecturer's podium, and a larger number of middle-sized rooms (seating 50 to 70), similarly designed with gently tiered arcs of bolted tables sloping down to a podium area. In these middle-sized rooms the lecturers stood in front of a system of screens and chalkboards designed for different kinds of visual presentations. There were televisions in almost every room (though I never saw or heard of them being used). Another wing of the building housed much smaller, brightly-lit classrooms ringing a wide hallway. Most of these rooms were furnished with small, movable (though never moved) tables big enough to sit two or three in comfortable, wicker-backed steel-framed chairs with cushioned seats.

Finally, there were windowless rooms, antiseptically white, set aside for computer use, filled with rows of white IBM personal computers in wooden carrels. These were usually used as adjunct classrooms where classes that might normally meet in regular classrooms would meet once a week to perform a computer analysis or participate in a simulation such as the B-game.

The organization of gaze was more variable in the business classrooms than in physics. The curvature of the seating in the larger rooms put the students in each other's lines of vision — another example of the display orientation of business school space. There were also differences in the ways faculty functioned as focal points in the classrooms. In physics one looked not so much at the professor as at what the professor was doing, the physics he unfolded, back to the students, on the chalkboards. The teacher was an adjunct to the material, an instrument for the conveyance of truths that belonged not to him, but that had an autonomous existence. In a sense what physics professors did was recreate the space of physics itself in the two-dimensional arena of the chalkboard; while students in turn recreated the professors' spatializations on the surface of their note-papers.

In business and especially management classes, by contrast, the professors were usually the focal points of the classrooms. Their classroom practice centerd around talk rather than writing. Students learned to gauge from the tone, tempo, and emphasis of the lecture what was 'important', what would appear on the test. The visual adjuncts that faculty used took the form of prepared displays, such as overhead projector transparencies, instead of creations unfolding in time, like the physics professors' board work. The visual displays supported and illustrated the professors' talk. Knowledge and expertise resided in the speaker, who was imparting *his* understanding rather than conveying 'absolute truths'. In Bourdieu's (1986) terms knowledge in physics was 'objectified', in management 'embodied'.

In their academic work students were correspondingly most concerned about what the particular professor would find acceptable, not what was 'right' or, as the physics students would say, what 'worked'. In this strip of conversation, taken from a group case analysis, Curtis and Dorothy debate how much explanation they need to support their recommendations — the debate is about how the professor will read the case analysis:

Curtis:　He's not gonna dig that deep.

Dorothy:　I mean, I know, but I mean but if he reads down here and he says 'you don't have any basis for making this statement', you know, 'you didn't support it.' Know what I'm saying?

Curtis:　'It'll reduce costs.' How about that? It'll decrease transportation costs. . . .

Dorothy:　Yeah, but it'll increase other costs.

Curtis:　But still, we have a basis, that's our basis, that it's gonna decrease costs. That's our basis for making the statement. He doesn't know what else we thought of, you know, that it might increase something else. [pause] And after reading ten papers, if he thinks, if he's gonna think about that — I mean. [pause]

In the cumulative course of the curriculum, Managerial Strategy, students themselves became, for a session or two at least, the focal points of the classrooms (something that never happened in physics classes). They were expected to display their own embodied knowledge in formal 'presentations' of cases to the rest of the class. As Sheena recalled, these presentations were sources of great stress:

We had to make a presentation in Managerial Strategy. We were the first group: I went up there — and I used to do this all the time in high school, but once you're out of practice you go up there and it's like 'HHHHHeloooo' — all of us were shaking. Every one of us did this. And we were talking, each group as they finished their presentation, they'd go out in the hall, 'Oh, I'm nervous, I wonder how we did', and everybody walks out and pats them on the back: 'you did fine, don't worry about it.' And, ah, it's different. Because, really, we haven't had to do this until . . . you take Managerial Strategy. Ah, in most of my other classes you just sit there and the teacher talks to you, you write it down, and you regurgitate to her back on paper. Or turn it around and twist it and see if you can understand the question (Sheena).

In these presentations it was not only *what* students said that was important but how they looked, presented themselves, and managed the questions and comments from professors and other students. In one class I spent time in, the professor cut students off in mid-sentence — no matter how cogent or well argued their presentation — if they went over the allotted time.

In other classes, dealing with questions from the class was an important part of the presentation. In some cases, students collaborated with each other to hold the floor and prevent their professors from intervening and confronting the presenters with demands for detail, vague queries ('I don't understand your sentence'), or flat contradictions ('No! They're very strong product-wise'). As Sheena put it:

You don't want [Dr X] asking you questions! . . . He'll throw you one from left field that you're not expecting. At least with the students you've got a general idea. They're on the same knowledge level as you are (Sheena).

In other classes, however, grading was competitive and students tried to show up the presenters (and thus win attention for themselves) by asking difficult questions or making critical comments.

Finally, in some classes professors manipulated the presentation formats to focus them less on content and more on students' interpersonal skills. Curtis, for example, told me about an integrative finance class he'd taken (very similar to Managerial Strategy) where the professor would regularly disrupt planned presentation: changing teams at the beginning of class, making team members switch with each other the parts of the presentation they'd prepared; forcing them to work people into the presentation on short notice; or even to make presentations using someone else's notes.

In all of these kinds of public performances students were expected to stay within the tight discourse parameters of corporate subordinates: don't challenge the professor, don't ask questions that advertise your ignorance, don't ask questions to generate discussion. When students occasionally went beyond these parameters the results were awkward silences. Dorinne, one of the two older students I interviewed who had full-time jobs and lived off campus, made good grades in her courses but didn't mimic corporate styles of dress or conversation. As a result, the other students treated her as an oddity.

I'll ask: 'doesn't it strike many of you how easily we conform to propaganda? Doesn't it scare any of you?' I asked that in class, and I got blank stares from about three-quarters of the class. Sometimes I feel that I don't really fit — I know I don't really fit in the business school (Dorinne).

Dorinne's outspokenness and sometimes unorthodox dress — I remember being in a large class on Ash Wednesday when she came into the classroom late with ashes on her forehead and most of the room turned around in their seats to stare at her — were unusual. Most students, knowing that they had yet to be judged on their suitability for employment, regulated their appearance and performance styles tightly.

A 'Street' Inside: Students in Public Spaces

Bodies themselves generate spaces, which are produced by and for their gestures (Lefebvre, 1991, p. 216).

The atmosphere of performance, of being on display in a public setting, pervaded the business school. In contrast to physics, which collapsed the world into its work space through powerfully reductive representational technologies, management organized space and time by stretching itself out in a sort of imperialistic way across material spaces to produce a very extensive social space. This was accomplished partly by the kind of inter-institutional architectural isomorphisms described earlier in this chapter, but it also required practitioners — mobile, stable, combinable practitioners — who could be sent out to 'practice' those spaces properly. When I say that performances were routinized I mean bodily practice, appearance and sociability, were being standardized and mobilized in disciplinary forms. Student associations were a critical medium for this process.

In the physics program students interacted with a stable block of fellow majors with whom they moved from class to class, studied with, and formed friendships. The management students I interviewed didn't move through their classes together or work together, and their friendship networks consisted of people from hometown schools who were attending the university, people they'd met in university dormitories, and their boyfriends or girlfriends — not their classmates. Where academic and social life merged for (the male) physics students, for management students 'business' activity was constructed as separate not only from 'the academic' but also from 'the personal'. Finally, although enrolment in management resembled that in physics in that it took place through a group medium, the nature of the groups and the enrolments were very different.

The requirement that management students take a lot of courses outside their major produced student groups that were more loosely organized than friendship networks. Students entering the business school found the social world of the college dominated by a wide range of organizations: from fraternities and sororities (whose memberships were dominated by the business students), to the business school 'service organizations' that did community work and orchestrated meetings between students and members of the business community, to the associations linked to particular majors (e.g., the management association, the marketing association), or particular areas of business (e.g., the International Association of Students of Business, Commerce and Economics). Unlike the work groups in physics, which were formed afresh by each class of students, the fraternities, sororities, and associations were stable entities that pre-existed the student cohorts that participated in them. Some were allocated cramped and shared office space within the building (near the student cafeteria), and all had glass enclosed display cases along one hallway to post notices, announcements, and so forth). The groups weren't creations of the program, they were independent networks of association that extended the business school space beyond the academic setting and connected it to the world of work. Almost all students joined or attended meetings of these groups at some point in their academic careers.

Students believed that job recruiters placed a premium on membership and activity in these organizations, and that by participating in them they could 'network' and make connections that would help them in their careers. The groups were important for recruitment — as forms of social certification — and also served as means of access to jobs and employers, as introductions to job networks. As Dell explained: 'Definitely one of the main advantages of [belonging to groups] is that it looks good to a future employer, I think, being involved, not just being a student' (cf. Dalton, 1959, p. 164). Other students had similar analyses:

> I'm in the management association and the marketing association here. I've also been in IASBCE, International Association of Students of Business, Commerce and Economics. But I was only in that for a semester.
> [*Nespor*: Why did you join those?]
> Well, I hate to say it, but a lot of it had to do with résumés. Towards the end you start thinking 'I've got to make that résumé look better.' And while that's not a very good reason for starting it, I've really enjoyed my experiences with these associations, and thought that they've been very beneficial. Although I didn't get into them for maybe the right reasons or whatever (Rhonda).

Sometimes membership could lead directly to a job:

> I found a lot of friends in the business school just because I think you're so aware of 'networking' (laughs). And you want to make these friends, and it's just something that you do consciously. . . . I joined

[the Management Association] because I was getting worried about getting a job and I wanted to have more contacts. And it worked. [The group's sponsor, an adjunct faculty member with good connections in the local job market] got me a job (Melinda).

As these comments suggest, students were encouraged to look at their everyday friendships and activities in terms of their business utility. One returning alumna espoused this orientation in a presentation to students in the Management Association:

Learn how to talk to other people. And I'm talking about people in your classes, people that you meet on airplanes. One job offer that I had was on an airplane coming back from another interview I had had. . . . When you go to parties, make a point of meeting people that you *don't* know. I know it's easy to feel comfortable with the group that you are with. But try to extend beyond that group and meet new friends, because you'll be amazed how that circle will widen each time. It's kind of like a pebble in a pond. It gets, concentric circles, get bigger and bigger and bigger. . . .

Be involved . . . [in] clubs, whether they're formal or informal groups, professional organizations . . . civic groups as well . . . even volunteer kinda groups. I'm involved in a United Action for the Elderly, and the Meals on Wheels Program, and I've met contacts through that. . . . The other area . . . is church. If you have an opportunity to regularly attend a church, you meet all kinds of folks through that (Brenda, a corporate officer and alumna speaking to the Management Student Association).

Many of the organizations' activities centered explicitly on making connections and learning job-getting skills:

I joined these clubs to learn things, not like for social reasons. . . . Like [in a service organization], you learn things that will help you in your business career. We have top business people come talk from all over. We fly them in and they speak to us and give us pointers. We have like executive cocktail parties. We don't drink at it but we have like 250 executives from all over fly in. We've had résumé workshops (Clara).

The things being mobilized here were bodies: textually in résumés certifying one's sociability (not to mention the business cards that allowed one to accumulate acquaintances), and physically in the executives and speakers brought in to interact with students. Students were also encouraged to make themselves physically mobile:

Relocate if necessary. If you have an opportunity for a good job but it means you have to leave friends, family, security, do it. I promise you, you will never be sorry. And I can say that from personal experience. . . . You develop yourself by doing that. You find out what your fibre is, and what you're made of. And, again, it's an opportunity to have contacts that you'll keep for the rest of your life (Corporate speaker to Management Association seminar).

The cultivation of expansive networks of acquaintance (Granovetter, 1983) allowed students to extend themselves across space, to regionalize themselves rather than localize themselves in tightly connected networks.[5] The message of promoting or marketing oneself across large regions of space was broadcast to students at mixers, placement office programs, 'career week' seminars and similar events that taught them how to dress and act in business environments, and by corporations themselves through campus speakers and workshops. The following pronouncements were fairly typical of such events:

Too many people looking for the same jobs . . . Competition for all of us. . . . *We'd like to suggest to you that . . . career planning skills, how to market yourself, how to sell yourself in a competitive environment, is as important as those skills that you're developing in your discipline* (From a seminar presentation to business students, sponsored by a major corporation and business magazine, emphasis added).

These 'skills' of self-marketing were forms of corporate sociability that the business school environment promoted in an unstated but powerful way though the organization of everyday activity as a *public* spectacle. Management students (and other business students) didn't huddle in corridors late at night to study like the physics students. Instead almost all business students spent a considerable amount of their day socializing and relaxing in the corporate-like ambience of the business building. As far as I could tell, this public side to their academic careers distinguished them from students in non-business programs, where programmatic activity — classes, labs, or study groups — took place in closed or controlled spaces.

The public space of the business school, as I've already suggested, was a stage for the display of one's embodied corporate competence. Dan Rose (1987), an ethnographer of urban street life, gives an account of the public 'street' in urban African-American culture that resonates with my own observations in the business school, with the students' comments on sociability, and with Jackall's descriptions of managerial practice:

The street was under constant surveillance, scanned, spied upon. It was fully filled in; everything was noticed, the least gesture attended to. It was a viscous gelatin of awareness. Walking down the block was extremely intense. The facades were alive through their apertures, and all who walked on the street felt they were in the theatre of total performance. People cut through the viscosity as they walked, or inhabited it as they left indelible, communal traces; they inscribed an aesthetic nuance with their gestures, their speech, their lives (Rose, 1987, p. 38).

We could think of this as a kind of 'panopticonism' (Foucault, 1979; Spain, 1992), but only by imagining a panopticon composed entirely of mirrors. As if on a street, students were on display throughout the business building, to look at and be seen by other students passing through the halls. This was true even in the bathrooms (at least the men's), which differed from those elsewhere on campus both in size (they were very large) and in the fact that each had one wall, across from the wash basins, covered with a full-sized mirror in front of which the young men preened and prepared themselves for re-entry into the public area. Students watched each other (and the faculty — one professor in particular was ridiculed for his thin wardrobe of acrylic sweaters), and faculty judged students, in a very general way (most management faculty never learned the names of individual students), on dress and demeanour.

Late in the semester, for example, waiting for class to begin in a Managerial Strategy course I'd been sitting in for the whole term, a day on which students would present research projects, the professor stopped to comment on the different ways students dressed and presented themselves: some elaborately done up, others extremely casual, wearing shorts, T-shirts, sandals (I never saw anyone in the B-school dressed *that* casually, but the first speaker in class that day did begin his presentation wearing a gimme-cap. The professor insisted he take it off). The professor argued that those who showed more consideration for their demeanour were more likely to be considerate and diligent on the job: appearance was a token of competence.

Dress and deportment were spatializing devices that allowed one to produce or accomplish business space, and to signify belonging to the business space, being a legitimate player in it (cf. Jackall, 1988, p. 47). Melinda, who'd begun college as a liberal arts major, explained:

> The business school is more formal. You'll find a totally different dress code in the business school. You walk into a business class and everybody's all dressed real nice, and you can point out the people that have interviews today. I used to have business classes on like Mondays, Wednesdays, and Fridays, and Liberal Arts classes on Tuesdays and Thursdays. And I would dress differently on those days. Ah, so there's a completely different feel. And for a person to realize that they don't fit into the business school, that would be important to learn that early before you get all caught up in that major (Melinda).[6]

Differences in the standards of dress for men and women reflected the 'genderedness' of managerial occupations, their association with 'masculinity' and the concomitant devaluation of traditionally 'feminine' styles of appearance. According to one corporate consultant: 'By way of nature and their conventional dress standards, women generally have a harder time looking professional' (Cox, 1986, p. 74). Physical 'attractiveness' (as defined by men) is a handicap for female aspirants to managerial positions (Heilman and Saruwati, 1979), and women in 'masculine' apparel seem to be more favourably rated by recruiters than women in 'feminine' apparel (Forsythe, Drake and Cox, 1985). Students may not have been conscious of the research underlying dress prescriptions, but they were usually aware of what was prescribed. If they weren't, they were told. One Placement Centre official recounted that 'a couple of semesters ago it seemed like nobody even knew how to dress. So we did 'How to Dress' workshops, you know, and brought in retailers and different things to give them examples of what they needed to wear.' One way or another, students were highly conscious of bodily expectations:

> It's something you look for even in your classes. You can tell who's interviewing that particular day because they have a maroon tie on, and a dark grey suit. Girls, females, are expected to wear blue suits. . . . Students are very aware of what the appropriate dress is. . . . When you go to a party and everyone else is standing there and you look different, it's pretty obvious what you need. There are seminars held in the business school on what appropriate dress is, what you're expected to wear or not. . . . You really do need to fit in. . . . Certainly, when you go to the cocktail parties, when you go to the recruiting functions, there's a certain way you have to act, and certain colours of suits, certain colours of ties, certain shoes you can wear. It's a very restrictive environment in a lot of ways (Doug).

Doug's analysis is echoed by Jackall's comments on managerial practice in the corporate world:

> In a world where appearances — in the broadest sense — mean everything, the wise and ambitious manager learns to cultivate assiduously the proper, prescribed modes of appearing. He dispassionately takes stock of himself, treating himself as an object, as a commodity. He analyzes his strengths and weaknesses and decides what he needs to change in order to survive and flourish in his organization. And then he systematically undertakes a program to reconstruct his image, his publicly avowed attitudes or ideas, or whatever else in his self-presentation that might need adjustment (Jackall, 1988, p. 59).

This conscious and strategic construction of bodies and bodily practices is not quite consistent with the position articulated, for example, by Bordo (1989), who, following Foucault (1979) suggests that:

Not chiefly through 'ideology', but through the organization and regulation of the time, space, and movements of our daily lives, our bodies are trained, shaped, and impressed with the stamp of prevailing historical forms of selfhood, desire, masculinity, femininity (p. 14).

This notion of 'docile bodies' may be misleading. By embracing it we limit our ability to conceive of and study the strategic self-constructions of powerful bodies (bodies of power?) that occupied the energies of both students and practitioners of management. Foucault and those who follow him on this point address only one side of Soja's (1989) 'socio-spatial dialectic': they ignore people's creative appropriations and reconstructive activities within material organizations of space-time, in particular the conscious manipulation of bodily organization.

Bourdieu's work is problematic for similar reasons. Parts fit well with my arguments: for example, the suggestion in Bourdieu and Boltanski (1978) that the modern corporation:

requires agents capable of conducting external public relations (with other businesses, the state administration, etc.) necessary to the operation of the large integrated firm and to the maintenance of its control over the market, and also the internal public relations by which, in normal times, the internal order of the business is maintained. . . . Their outstanding qualities become an aptitude for discussion and negotiation, a knowledge of foreign languages and, perhaps especially, civilised and subtle manners . . . the new style of sociability objectively required by the changes in the economic field . . . all aspects of existence of the new managers, from their consumer habits to their day-to-day ethics or even their physical appearance, a sign of a new relation to the body (pp. 204–5).

But Bourdieu insists that the 'principles' embodied in dress, bearing, physical and verbal manners, are:

beyond the grasp of consciousness, and hence cannot be touched by voluntary, deliberate transformation, cannot even be made explicit; nothing seems more ineffable, more incommunicable, more inimitable, and therefore, more precious, than the values given body, *made* body by the transubstantiation achieved by the hidden persuasion of an implicit pedagogy, capable of instilling a whole cosmology, an ethic, a metaphysic, a political philosophy, through injunctions as insignificant as 'stand up straight' or 'don't hold your knife in your left hand' (1977, p. 94).

The insistence that notions such as 'embodied cultural capital' and 'habitus' (Bourdieu, 1977; 1986) can only refer to unconscious dispositions outside the control and manipulation of the actor limits their value (Moerman, 1989; de Certeau, 1984). As Jackall (1988) argues:

> the notion of cultural capital is a concept that may obscure more than it reveals about managers' actual social world while adding little to one's real understanding of what makes that world work. . . . Managers, at least American managers,[7] tend to think about the matter differently. They recognize, of course, the crucial importance of social breeding, particularly exposure to the proper social manners that the right schools afford. But one can try to acquire the 'right style' by altering one's personality through self-rationalization. In any event, one does not accumulate style (p. 214).

In other words, a regime of bodily practice or sociability, a style, embodied but not contained in the body (rather, distributed across the network of dress, people and material spaces in which people interact) can be consciously and strategically assumed by management students within the material spaces of the business school.

Clothing, gestures, and the like, weren't simply 'markers' (Goffman, 1971) of a corporate sociability, they were integral to its production. Again, there is an analogy to the life on the urban street described by Rose (1987):

> Clothing was worn like a mask — a mask not of concealment but of revelation. It was a statement or indicator, not just of self in some abstract way, but of where one wanted to appear as a performer in the public staging. . . . Clothing makes the man; the logic, according to Tom, was that if one presented a finely turned out version of oneself and was made social by it, one became, *behind that* (as a result of), ambitious. In other words, one would have performance possibilities to live up to (p. 174).

Compare Jackall's words:

> managers also suspect that clothes and grooming might indeed make the man. . . . Proper management of one's external appearances simply signals to one's peers and to one's superiors that one is prepared to undertake other kinds of self-adaptation (Jackall, 1988, p. 47).

Part of what distinguishes the street inside from the street outside is that corporate spaces are connected across time and space in a much more stable network than urban streets. The people Rose (1987) studied built spatial structures that had to be reconstructed daily and thus were localized to the community of immediate co-participants. The end of performance was the creation of a distinctive 'personal' identity. By contrast, the corporate practice management students were moving towards involved explicitly formalized and ritualized body styles and modes of interaction that made the bodies of practitioners much more stable and mobile across corporately organized spaces — and thus more easily connected or 'combined' with those of others (cf. Collins', 1979, discussion of 'formal culture').[8] The business school environment was a practice space for corporate appearance and behaviour and thus a site for students to begin mobilizing and stabilizing their bodies and bodily practices.

If students were occasionally loose in how they dressed for class they were almost never so when encountering corporate representatives. We've already seen that this happened occasionally in meetings of student associations, mixers, and so forth. One place where such meetings invariably happened for business students was in the job interview.

The Interview as a Display Space

Listen intently. When ready to answer a question, it is sometimes effective to take a moment or two to ponder an answer. It will make you look thoughtful and make your answers appear more meaningful and less as if they have been prepared in advance, which, of course, they have been (Stewart and Faux, 1979, p. 239).

The recruiting interview was a kind of trial-by-interaction. It was more important to getting hired, students argued, than grades. Clara reflected the common wisdom of students that '[recruiters] would first look at the interview . . . and then look at your Grade Point Average (GPA) and activities and stuff like that. But I think that the interview is the most important thing.' Of course, many firms used GPAs to limit the size of the applicant pool and select the students they would interview, but Clara's insistence on the interview's importance was frequently repeated, and not just by students. A speaker at the corporate sponsored seminar on 'career skills', drew an analogy between dress and deportment in an interview and the presentation of a product in a television commercial:

I'm going to draw the parallel between the interview and a commercial. . . . We have to express ourselves, express our interests, express our accomplishments — basically, express what we're all about in a period of eight minutes. . . . A very limited amount of time. Just as a commercial. Believe it or not, the first ten seconds of the interview is when you make your most lasting impression. . . . What can you do to best sell yourself within ten seconds? . . . appearance. You can look the part. Which doesn't necessarily mean your grays and your blues. . . . smile is key, as well as, as well as eye contact . . . it makes you very uncomfortable, somebody who can't establish that eye contact immediately . . . because it helps to develop that positive first rapport with the interviewer. . . . Right level of assertiveness, which includes . . . the handshake with the interviewer.[9]

Skills of self-presentation were critical in setting the tone of the interviewing and framing the recruiter's interpretation of what transpired in the remainder of the interview (Motowidlo, 1986). Like the speaker just quoted, recruiters brought in to speak to the Management Student Association claimed that decisions were frequently made within the first minute of an interview: 'first impressions are the most important', one put it, 'the handshake might be the most important thing you do' (cf. Buckley and Eder, 1988; Springbett, 1958).

There was a fairly elaborate system in place to prepare students for these encounters. The placement office stocked 'how-to' guides on job hunting and a library of information on corporations. Counsellors provided students with tests and self-administered questionnaires that assessed their wants, interests and goals and thus helped them present themselves more effectively to recruiters. Students were reminded that they didn't really know what they wanted to do in life; that their 'goals', like their outward appearance, had to be consciously molded. As one speaker to the Management Student Association, a recruiter for a large high-tech firm, remarked to the assembled students:

Here's the most difficult task for you to accomplish: have a goal . . . make a stab at coming up with a goal, and *write it down*. You hear that all the time. And I thought, 'write it down, I mean, what's the big deal?' When you write it down you make a commitment to yourself, on that sheet of paper, that this is what this is gonna be all about, and you tend to follow through with it a lot better. And you tend to not get so confused along the way (Brenda, a corporate officer and alumna speaking to the Management Student Association).

In addition to coaching students in the technologies of constructing appropriate goals and interests, the preparation system also provided students with more mundane resources. The placement office, for example, had guidelines, examples, and templates for writing résumés (including a list of over 200 'action words' — verbs to be used in describing one's experiences in the résumé), cover letters, letters requesting an interview, thank you letters, letters acknowledging or accepting a job offer, letters refusing an offer, lists of questions most likely to be asked in interviews, 'questions you can ask in an interview', and 'tips on interviewing' (listing 41 sins that can 'kill your chance for success' in an interview: 40 of the 41 dealt with appearance or interactional style problems). Almost all of the management students had used these resources by their senior year, and some applied them in detail. Curtis, for example, explained:

I have those . . . '50 questions interviewers like to ask' [a handout obtained from the placement center] — I go with those. And I think how I'm going to answer those, most of them, not quite all of them . . . I go over these questions and that's basically it. It covers pretty much the whole sheboom. And then also, I try to write down a few questions

I want to ask them. And that's the main thing. . . . Some of those questions are pretty deep, pretty hard to answer. Like the first two: 'What are your objectives for the next five years?' Long range objectives . . . This [the handout] covers pretty much anything they would ask, although I have heard of the, ah, 'interview hints', like in the placement manual [He shows me the manual]. They have some hints in there, like 'Look them in the eye and lean forward', you know, that sort of thing. But I've kind of learned that after a little experience it makes it pretty easy.

In fact, though, depending entirely on books or guide sheets to help one consciously mold one's body and bodily practices was problematic. Curtis, of whom I saw a good deal in the spring semester when he was interviewing, could *explain* how one successfully interviewed, but he didn't *do* it (and was seemingly unaware of the fact). He wore off-the-rack suits that didn't hang right and his personal mannerisms, at least in his academic classes (I never saw him interview) were immodest, or to use the phrasing of the placement center's sin list: 'overbearing-overaggressive-conceited-'superiority complex'-know-it-all' (Sin # 2). As a student who worked with him in the managerial strategy class remarked to me once, he was a show-off, and 'members don't usually sit around recounting personal triumphs.' Throughout the spring, he was stuck with a string of interviews for jobs he didn't want (e.g., in sales) with relatively undesirable firms.

A number of students told me that, as Curtis's case suggests, the resources in the placement center were worth using, but had essential limitations:

Well, really, I've found it difficult to prepare for an interview, because if you don't know — like you said, looking at the questions they give you from the placement center, nine times out of ten those questions aren't asked anyway, so really, just trying to stand on my feet the best I can. I try to think as quickly as possible (Jack).

Like Jack, Rhonda argued that books were no substitute for the experience of interviewing:

There's so much written on the subject [of interviewing] — but basically if you read a couple of articles or books or whatever, it starts repeating the same things. And I think, as far as answering questions and things like that, ah, practice. That's the only way to feel comfortable in situations.

'Practicing' interviews was a way for students to gain experience in the control of demeanor and proper interactional technique. They did this by setting up appointments with recruiters from companies that they weren't really interested in working for. Although students had to know something about the firm they interviewed with to ask appropriate questions, the questions *they* would be asked by recruiters were so standardized that interviewing with one firm could be a useful preparation for an interview with another firm, even if the two companies were in different industries. Although placement officers frowned on this practice of 'practicing', students were encouraged to do it by both advisers and peers:

> I'm one of those terrible people that will tell you to interview for interview's sake. The Placement people hate me 'cause, hey, I'm the one that helps jam up those lists [laughs] and the lines start forming all the way down, and every time something comes up where they sort through all the résumés, boy, mine was in there, it was in the box (Brenda, a corporate officer and alumna speaking to the Management Student Association).

The practice interviews gave students opportunities to develop self-confident and smooth interactional styles. One had to be able to present a self that refused to admit any weaknesses or uncertainties but simultaneously re-frained from boasting of strengths. As Brenda explained, interviewees get in trouble when 'they don't come across as themselves. . . . And people in an interview spot that, like that! So, be yourself, and be confident about who you are.' But being yourself was a complicated balancing act that involved, in Brenda's words, 'stretching but not lying' about your competencies. How should one respond to questions like — Are you creative? Are you analytical? Are you a leader? — with firm and assured modesty. How do you negotiate the common 'knock-out' factor of lacking well-defined goals and a career plan? By excising all the modalities of desire and need that make one less mobile in corporate space. When I asked Bart about his goals he struggled to articulate them:

> Well, I have to consider my wife when I make goals, but I guess we're kind of traditional. We've got your American dream. I don't want to be stagnant in my career, but I'd like to not have to move around a lot. And that's asking a lot these days. But if I could just get myself in a situation where I could see where I had the opportunity to go, as far as moving up the career ladder, I wouldn't mind settling down and getting a house with some land. We're both real family-oriented. So where we could raise a family and still spend time seeing our family and friends. But then again I would have my career as far as what I want to do with my career. If I can see where I have a chance to go it won't get too redundant on me to be in one position for a good while. As long as I know I can move up in my career. I'd like to settle down as far as geography goes. So I guess that's our long-term goals. Raise a family. I don't know.

When I asked him how he would have answered that question if I'd been a corporate interviewer asking it, his reply omitted all the concerns of his original answer and put in their place the thin logic of a corporate trajectory:

> I have been asked that question, like 'in five years, where do you see yourself?' I'll say, 'moving into a middle management position.' Which is what I want to do, but, I wouldn't say 'I want to be CEO in ten years so watch out.' Just to be in a position where I can move upwards, upwards without having to move away.

Be ambitious but not too ambitious. The truly proficient practitioner of corporate sociability, at least by one account, would never deviate from the studied norms of bland pleasantness. A corporate-sponsored speaker advised students to:

> Be professional, and polite, to each and every person along the way. Which includes secretaries. Secretaries oftentimes can play a very key role in whether or not you're hired for the position. Be polite to everybody along the way, from the person who you're walking next to along the street, to the person who you ride up the elevator with. You never know who that little man is over there in the corner of the elevator (Corporate-sponsored seminar).

It's hard to argue with the notion that we should be nicer to secretaries, but what's being advocated, I think, is less a common civility than a strategic, self-monitored performance of 'professionalism': personality without the modalities of humour, passion, desire or conscience. Talking of bodies and social practices in this way presumes a vision of them as malleable constructions constituted and articulated through 'semiotic-material' (Haraway, 1991) systems: dress, toilet, material settings, the regulation of the kinds of people one interacts with, interaction settings, the foods and drugs one ingests — all of these codified in relatively explicit ways that stabilize them and make them mobile within networks of corporate practice.

This interplay of body and space in the business school is a complex one. Corporate space itself reflects a shift 'from the space of the body to the body-in-space (Lefebvre, 1991, p. 196), a 'decorporealization' of space that produces an 'abstract' 'space dominated by the eye and the gaze' (Gregory, 1994, p. 392). Of course, something similar could be said for physics as well, but in physics abstract space was a construction on paper, a way of making distant and invisible things visible, close, and pliable. In management, abstract space was a material organization of space-time, a way of making close and contextualized things visible, distant and mobile. The body became a spatially organized construction taking form as a conjunction of somatic and extra-somatic flows within standardized display spaces woven across settings of corporate education and practice.

The undergraduate management program, instead of connecting students to a network of practices for mobilizing and compressing the world into a central setting, prepared students to go out towards the distant centers of the corporate network. Whereas the physics program was tightly attached to a core site of practices for mobilizing the physical world, the management program was one of many mobilized settings for corporate actor-networks. In the former students 'learned' by making things move, in the latter by making themselves mobile.

Notes

1 There are, of course, any number of mathematized representations in management — 'Return on Assets', etc. — but the management students I talked to did very little with such formulas. Even in their final, senior year courses they had to flip back to textbook appendices to remind themselves of the exact nature of the formulas; and they *used* the formulas only when directed by professors. I'll stress, however, that I am talking about *management* majors here. The situation may have been very different, and more similar to physics, in a field like accounting or operations management.

2 I mention the art — there was a lot of it and the pieces seemed to have been bought in part for their size (all were *big*) — in part because of the parallels with the corporate workplace and in part because it set the business building apart from others on campus, none of which had art collections like this (at best, portraits of the people the buildings were named after or some reproductions hung up in office areas).

3 Academic faculty were also socially distanced from 'practical' faculty. The instructors and adjunct faculty were scattered around the complex in small offices, without secretarial buffers, close to or in student areas of the building (adjunct faculty, in fact, had offices in rooms that seemed to be originally designed as interviewing rooms for corporate recruiters).

4 The advisers in physics, by contrast, were in offices that opened directly into public hallways. Their doors were not closed when the adviser was present, and students simply walked in unless (and sometimes in spite of the fact that) the adviser was already engaged. Moreover, the undergraduate adviser in physics did not evaluate, but instead handled scheduling problems, finding students internships in professor's labs, etc.

5 Contrast this to the intrinsically *local* modes of association — the tight friendship networks — among working class European-Americans, Hispanics or African-Americans described by Willis (1981), Foley (1990) or Rose (1987). This is not an exclusive opposition, however. As we saw with physics, extremely localized groups can be extremely powerful to the extent that they are able to mobilize large parts of experience and collapse it into their local space. Using Goffman's (1971) terms, we could say that the management program, and corporate practice generally, marginalize 'anchored ties' while creating dense webs of 'anonymous' ties. 'Personal identity' doesn't disappear, but it is pushed into the corners and 'social identities' take center stage. In physics, by contrast, personal and social identities are collapsed into one.

6 I dressed differently when I went to the business school as well. If I went into physics or sociology areas wearing a suit and carrying a briefcase I'd be pegged as a textbook salesman. But without the accoutrements — and this was a very long

time before I began to think in terms of the analysis I'm developing in this chapter — I felt out of place in the Business School Building, obvious, awkward. I started carrying around a tie and fresh shirt in my attaché case and always went straight to the men's room to freshen up when I came to the B-School from another part of campus. While bodily appearance is hardly the whole story of mobilizing oneself for a corporate trajectory it's a *sine qua non*. I once interviewed for a job with the educational division of Arthur Andersen and without exception, the first thing I was told when I talked to someone was that I'd really have to shave my beard (I didn't get offered the job).

7 The qualifier is important. Business schools play a much more important role in the United States than in France (Marceau, 1979). In other words, 'cultural capital' may be less malleable in France than in the United States.

8 There are several advantages for core firms in an economy in having employees who share attributes and interpersonal and communicative styles geared to the demands and practices of the organization. They allow the rapid translation of external events into the operating vocabulary of the organization (March and Simon, 1958), make possible the rapid and accurate transmission of information across large, geographically fragmented social networks (Kanter, 1977, p. 57), and facilitate group formation and action by signalling status group co-membership (Collins, 1979, p. 61).

9 These seminars were presented by relatively young men and women (in their 20s) who performed skits of interviews and such in addition to talking to the people attending. There were also brief video presentations on various issues (the videos slipping in generous references to the products of the sponsoring corporations). I'd emphasize the fact that the presenters were *not* business people, nor, in the case of the one fellow I talked to, graduates of business schools: he was an actor. The point is that the sociability being conveyed was explicitly a performance, a simulation.

Chapter 6

Knowledge in Motion

Spatial and temporal practices are never neutral in social affairs.
They always express some kind of class or other social content, and
are more often than not the focus of intense social struggle (Harvey,
1989, p. 239).

Declaring that knowledge and learning are space-time processes is a way of
detaching them from the discourse of psychology and connecting them to
debates in social theory. Assumptions from both psychology and social theory
get disturbed along the way. This chapter summarizes that disruption, examines
its relevance and value, and looks forward to its implications.

The question that framed this study was how schooling activities are
connected to activities in other settings. In traditional psychological accounts
activites are presumed to be connected by individuals who, possessing some
sort of generative capacity (e.g., cognitive schemata, habitus), have that capacity altered at one point in time [in school], and carry with them the consequences of those alterations to their practices in settings encountered at points
later in time.

By focusing on spatiality I've tried to disrupt these assumptions. If it is not
clear by now, let me emphasize again that I'm interested in spatiality and
temporality as constructed spaces and times, constructed through networks of
relationships connecting animate and inanimate objects combined and arrayed
across vastly separated contexts. I am not using 'space' metaphorically, nor am
I merely saying that since everything happens in space, then so must 'learning'. I'm saying that people move through space materially, and simultaneously move and construct space-time through practices of representation, and
that what we call 'learning' are segments of motion which follow the shapes
of more stable institutional or disciplinary networks.

Institutional settings and activities aren't arrayed chronologically in time
(from the perspective of the individual), but in networks that construct space-
time relations. Participants in one part of a network are always interacting with
the other parts of the network, though the interactions are often asymmetrical
and unequal. Students in the undergraduate programs weren't being prepared,
or preparing themselves, to participate *later* in professional fields of practice;
they *were* interacting with those fields.

From this perspective, 'learning' is, first, being able to move oneself and, second, other things through those space-time networks. If the phrase 'having knowledge' means anything it means participating in an actor-network that organizes a field of practice such as a 'discipline' (although that is only one example — unions, community organizations, and so on could also function as actor-networks). Participating means becoming spatially and temporally organized in a form that moves you into the material spaces of the field, and becoming proficient at using the discipline's representational organizations of space-time. The 'discipline' itself exists as a stable entity insofar as it ties together spaces and times, mobilizes elements, and moves them across the distances to a center where they can be combined and acted upon. Some college programs are both components of disciplinary networks in this sense, as well as sites for reproducing disciplinary practitioners. The programs I studied were sites where people were connected, albeit in subordinate ways, to networks of power that organized activity in crucial parts of the everyday world. To understand learning and knowledge it's just as essential to trace out the network structures and the political economy that sustains them as it is to study students' experiences in specific settings of pedagogy or practice. The programs are not different 'levels' of a process but different regions of a complex, highly interactive network.

Although it owes much to theories of 'situated learning' (e.g., Lave, 1988; Lave and Wenger, 1991), the argument I'm advancing differs fundamentally in its insistence on attention to the spatio-temporal mobilizations that bring those different regions of networks into articulation. The preoccupation of situated learning theories with apprenticeship models and practices in small-scale craftwork communities suggests a kind of nostalgia for localized, pre-capitalist forms of social organization. Activity is presumed to take place in circumscribed, bounded settings among practitioners linked by strong social ties. The key notion of community seems of a piece with the Heideggerian notion of 'place', glossed by Doreen Massey (1993) as that of a clearly bounded setting with an essential identity 'constructed out of an introverted, inward-looking history based on delving into the past for internalized origins' (p. 64). The results are limiting conceptualizations of setting, activity, participation and identity. Power drops out of the analysis, history is reduced to the life cycle of the local community.

In contrast, I have argued that schooling (or any other setting or 'community of practice') can't be understood on its own terms, but only by looking at how its practices are enmeshed in much more expansive networks. Schooling isn't a mere reflection of 'larger' processes — economic, political, or whatever — nor does it 'produce' (or reproduce) those processes. One part of a network doesn't create another, but lines of connection and the people and things flowing through them are always under stresses, always contested. Things are defined by their connections. Places are constructions made up of other spaces that have been mobilized and circulated through networks distributed across, and constituting, spaces and times. 'Face-to-face' interaction is a misnomer: in addition to people and things in the immediate setting people are always interacting with *distant* entities that have been materially or semiotically trans- ported into the encounter.[1]

Once we see the world as laced together through space-time compression and processes of distanciation, questions of power become unavoidable. I showed in chapters 2 to 5 how the physics and management programs simul- taneously concentrated student activity within bounded material organizations of space-time *and* began to link those students (albeit in very different ways) to distant sites of disciplinary practice through representational organizations of space-time. The programs were one articulation of a process in which centers of power become concentrated in small, densely organized places scattered around the globe but connected to each other by flows of represen- tations through the disciplinary web. This 'simultaneous, flexible process of centralizing and decentralizing activities' (Castells, 1991a, p. 14) is character- istic of global economies, where the 'territorial dispersal of . . . economic activ- ity creates a need for expanded central control and management' (Sassen, 1992, p. 4). These are necessary conditions for sustaining a globally dispersed elite and generating spatio-temporal boundaries separating that elite from other groups. As Castells (1991) suggests:

> The new professional-managerial class colonizes exclusive spatial segments that connect with one another across the city, the country, and the world; they isolate themselves from the fragments of local societies, which in consequence become destructured in the process of selective reorganization of work and residence (Castells, 1991, p. 348).

The dispersed centers of power are connected in representational organ- izations of space-time that tie together what Castells refers to as 'spaces of flows'. Indeed, the power of the centers depends on their being able to con- stitute a space of flows that ties them together while localizing and fragment- ing other regions of activity. The centralizing and decentralizing features of modern social organization (the material and representational organizations of space-time, respectively) are created and sustained through the activities of actor-networks. These networks revolve around the work of mobilizing the world so that it can be moved through a space of flows, and so that elements of the networks, including students, physicists and managers, can themselves move through those spaces in one form or another. Disciplinary learning and knowledge are forms of motion through representational organizations of space, spaces of flows.

The physics and management students, by attaching themselves to actor- networks and participating in their practices of representation, were becoming participants in the control and manipulation of disciplinary flows. Physics pro- duced a material organization of space-time where students were concentrated and linked to other practitioners and settings of physics by a space of flows that reduced the natural world to texts and machines. Management produced a space of place that mimicked but sharply distinguished itself from professional workspaces; a space of flows in which the self became a flow.

'Selves' are not simply multiplied or fragmented, they're distributed across space-time networks, constituted in their material and semiotic connections. Different disciplinary constructions of space and time mean different constructions of self.[2] The physics program compressed students' spatial and temporal activity, bent them into the discipline in a way that transformed them into dense integrated selves defined by small, close-knit networks of immediate peers, but *also* tightly linked to distant and unknown others participating in the same actor-network. The management program spread students out and segmented their practice into discrete frames of reference and hence different organizations of self, but their disciplinary selves were mobile bundles of social practices that allowed them to move in and out of distant business settings, at least provisionally.

Making other things mobile and acting upon them in your setting, and moving yourself from one powerful setting to another, are characteristics of the disciplinary power that the physics and management students were becoming participants in. As Doreen Massey (1993) puts it, there is a 'power-geometry' to the space of flows: 'different social groups and different individuals are placed in very distinct ways in relation to these flows and interconnections' (p. 61):

> mobility and control over mobility both reflect and reinforce power. It is not simply a question of unequal distribution, that some people move more than others, some have more control than others. It is that the mobility and control of some groups can actively weaken other people (Massey, 1993, p. 62).

This idea of a power-geometry to the organization of space is another way of making the point that the mobilizations of students in the disciplinary network are constitutive of power relations, not just incidentally connected to them. It isn't so much position as the pattern of movement, knowledge in motion, that defines power relations. These different regimes of motion build on and create social divisions that are rooted in differential experiences of space and time. As Pred and Watts (1992) summarize this argument:

> In [Castells and Henderson's (1987)] language, one fundamental aspect of the 'internationalization of techno-economic processes' is the tendency for the 'space of flows to supersede the space of places' (p. 7). Deleuze and Guattari (1977) refer to this sort of phenomenon as 'deterritorialization', in which the actual dynamics of a given location rely on, and are shaped by, activities and forces that are decidedly non-local. The logic and dynamics of territorial development are increasingly placeless. Yet at the same time, social relations, and much

of what passes as everyday life, continue to operate according to a local, place-oriented logic (the 'space of places') (pp. 11–12).

As Castells (1991) himself puts it, 'People live in places, power rules through flows' (p. 349). This produces a 'schizophrenia', he argues, 'between the spatial frame of reference of the dominant elite and the spatial experience of most people who are rooted in their communities' (Castells, 1991a, p. 19). The result is a dramatic weakening of the possibilities for communication, cooperation or conflict.

How can a flow relate to a neighbourhood meeting or to the formation of culture on a playground? There is no relation, there is no communication. The process of disintegrating society starts at that point, because people are not enemies, but aliens (Castells, 1991a, p. 19).

If physics and management students were becoming 'alien' to people like me and others outside their fields it wasn't because they were being swallowed up in disciplinary apparatuses or having their lifeworlds colonized (to use Habermas's phrase); it was because they were moving in space-times that the rest of us don't — and increasingly can't — move in.

Castells qualifies his bleak portrait, but his general message is cautionary. Space-time compression and the globalization of economic and cultural flows create fragmenting pressures and disrupt communication among groups differently positioned and mobilized in the power-geometry. As we have seen in this book, disciplines are implicated in this process as they organize space and time in distinctive ways closed to outsiders. As educational practices play key roles in moving students into these spaces and times and in creating the boundaries that separate insiders and outsiders, the study of learning and knowledge can't be separated from the study of the organization of the social world, which includes its spatialities and temporalities. As Gupta and Ferguson (1992) remark:

We need to theorize how space is being *re*territorialized in the contemporary world. . . . Physical location and physical territory, for so long the *only* grid on which cultural difference could be mapped, need to be replaced by multiple grids that enable us to see that connection and contiguity — more generally the representation of territory — vary considerably by factors such as class, gender, race and sexuality, and are differently available to those in different locations in the field of power (p. 20).

And I would push this further. Since our research, theorizing, and writing are contributions to flows of information, and hence make us participants in the reterritorializations our works comment on, we're obliged to take responsibility for the politics that can be accomplished through our works.

A lot of educational research tells the stories of groups that have been discriminated against or disadvantaged by the schools; groups localized, immobilized, or mobilized to serve the needs of more powerful groups. Such research conjures up the political agenda of critical social science (Fay, 1988). It holds the promise of raising consciousness, explaining to oppressed groups the conditions of their oppression, and giving them a theory and praxis to lead them out of that oppression. Although such works often move within a spatialization that keeps them separate from their intended audiences, hence vitiating their politics, the intended logic of the research enterprise is clear.

The logic of the present work may be less obvious. I've 'studied up' to examine the educational constructions of 'powerful' learners. My aim is not to raise the students' consciousness or move them to action (they have a good understanding of their programs); nor is my aim to improve pedagogy in the fields (for, despite occasional doubts voiced by educators in the fields, the programs do pretty well what they're intended to do). In fact, some of the arguments I've advanced in this book could be taken as explanations for why it won't have much impact as an intervention in physics or management practice. Action moves through space-time networks and the book moves in a different spatial and temporal frame of reference than physics or management practice. Its effects will probably be confined to the network within which it mobilizes educational portions of the physics and management networks: educational research.

What the book offers for educational studies is a re-territorialization that rejects the boundaries commonly drawn around institutions, communities and activities. Instead, the focus is on what's getting mobilized, how it circulates, who accumulates it where, and how this motion defines and connects things as it shapes spatial and temporal relations.

To do this right probably means re-casting research as a multi-researcher multi-site engagement. Most actor-networks will be much harder to study than disciplinary settings like the physics and management programs. And it hasn't escaped me that my own spatiality in this study was highly localized: ideally there should have been multiple case studies of different regions or positions in the disciplinary networks, studies of the different ways of moving through them. It'll be difficult to organize this kind of work unless it has a clearer link to, and a clearer political engagement with the groups whose space and time we, as researchers and writers, participate, albeit in subordinate ways, in shaping.

Such engagement means thinking about how others can get involved in producing representational organizations of space-time, how the geometry of flows can be reconfigured so that formerly marginalized sites can become nodes and centers of accumulation as well; how participation can be maximized. I don't mean to suggest that these are questions we should ask *in* our research. I mean that our work, not so much how we write, but how what we write moves, implicates us in answers to these questions.

The coupling of knowledge and power is something more than a rhetorical assertion: it's an empirical question of how material spaces are constructed or regionalized, how people move in and out of them and within them; how the world is mobilized, where it's collected, and who acts upon it. Physics and management education resolve these issues in ways that allow them to assemble widespread and stable networks that shape and affect large regions of human experience. What sort of networks do we as educational researchers build? How might we reshape them?

Notes

1   Notions such as 'intertextuality' or 'heteroglossia' assume distanced interactions, but ignore the question of mechanisms — the networks that organize space and time. In fact, they are grounded in the particular networks of — and reflect an unacknowledged universalization of the position of — academic, university-based readers.
2   One problem with the Lave and Wenger (1991) framework is that it takes as its model seemingly localized and isolated fields of practice and treats them as exemplars of all practice.

Appendix 1

The Place of the Major

This appendix explains my decision to focus on courses in the major field of study rather than non-major or 'general distribution' courses. For the reader unfamiliar with physics and management programs, Tables 1 and 2 reproduce the official course requirements for degrees in the fields.

It's clear that this book has focused on a particular portion of students' trajectories through the course requirements: for physics students their physics and math courses, for management students their business and management courses. Ignoring the 'general education' courses and non-specialization electives isn't unproblematic, but it does mimic the practice of the students themselves, all but a few of whom described such courses as distractions. In analyzing a year's worth of transcripts of recent physics and management graduates and in interviewing students nearing graduation, I found that students took their general distribution courses at various points in their college careers and imported many of them from other (usually less demanding) institutions such as community colleges. As a result, courses in the major were spatially localized and temporally sequenced in distinctive ways while courses outside the major were not.

Spatial and Temporal Dispersion of the Non-Major Courses

Many specific courses were required in the student's major field of study, but students had a great deal of discretion in where and when they took their general distribution courses. The transcripts reveal a spatial scattering of students' non-major coursetaking. Although they got their degrees from one university, their academic careers crossed many institutions. Over 86 per cent of all the students in the transcript sample had transferred hours from other universities, and over 54 per cent had taken thirty-one or more hours at other colleges (i.e., in excess of one full-year-equivalent of courses). As I've already suggested, the transfer hours were not randomly distributed across types of courses, but were concentrated in distribution or non-major coursework (see Table 3).

Most of the transfer hours in physics were the result of students beginning their studies at other universities or in other majors, transfer hours in management were more often the result of students strategically taking courses at other, less academically demanding institutions. Only three of the management

Table 1: Administrative Requirements for the Physics Major

Distribution Requirements (40 hours total)
  9 hours of English: 'Freshman Composition', 'Masterworks of Literature', and 'Writing in Different Disciplines'
  6 hours of American Government
  6 hours of American History
  13 hours in a foreign language
  3 semester hours from one of the following: anthropology, economics, geography, linguistics, psychology, sociology
  3 semester hours from one of the following: art, drama, music, classics, architecture, philosophy

Related Math and Science Requirements (37 hours total)
  24 hours in mathematics, at the calculus level and above
  8 hours of introductory chemistry
  5 hours of biological and/or geological science, including laboratory

Required Physics Courses (minimum of 40 hours)
  12 hours of lower division courses in physics:
    Wave Motion and Optics (with lab) (4 hours)
    Introductory Electricity and Magnetism (with lab) (4 hours)
    Introductory Mechanics (with lab) (4 hours)
  28 hours of upper division courses in physics, including:
    Classical Dynamics 1
    Classical Electrodynamics
    Introduction to Quantum Phenomena
    Applications of Quantum Mechanics
    Subatomic Physics
    Thermodynamics and Statistical Mechanics
    Quantum Mechanics
    Advanced Laboratory I

Recommended physics courses:
  Electronics Techniques (a 3 hour upper division course)
  Introductory Physics: (a 3 hour lower division course, not counting towards the BS)
  Introductory Physics Seminar (a 1 hour lower division course, not counting towards the BS)

---

students interviewed for this study had been at the university throughout their academic careers. Of the others, one transferred to the university with about one year of coursework left so she could get her degree from a more prestigious institution than the one she'd begun at. Three others, all women, moved from institution to institution following husbands or boyfriends.

For the rest, movement across institutions was strategic: spending a year at a community or junior college to get distribution requirements (mainly liberal arts courses such as English, history, government, but also some of the initial business requirements such as math, accounting and economics) out of the way at institutions that were both cheaper and easier than the university (Clara, for example, took 24 hours a semester at a community college, worked part-time, and maintained a 4.0 grade point average). Other students chose to avoid the very large and impersonal lower-division classes in math, economics and accounting, English, government and history, and instead took such classes at easier community colleges near home during the summer.

Table 2: Administrative Requirements for the Management Major

Distribution Requirements (60 hours total)
3 hours of English: 'Freshman Composition', 'Masterworks of Literature'
8 hours Business Calculus
3 hours of psychology or sociology
6 hours in fine arts or humanities: archaeology, architecture, art, classics, music, philosophy, Greek, Latin, drama, fine arts.
6 hours in the natural sciences: astronomy, biology, botany, microbiology, zoology, chemistry, geology, physics
6 hours of American Government
6 hours in American History
3 hours in 'applied communications' (from a college-approved list, including courses in media, journalism, and languages)
3 hours of upper-division business electives
6 hours of upper-division social science
At least 7 additional hours outside the College of Business Administration

Business Courses (39 hours)

Introduction to Macroeconomics	Introduction to Microeconomics
Financial Accounting	Managerial Accounting
Introduction to Data Processing	Business Statistics
Introduction to Business Law	Money and Banking
Principles of Marketing	Business Finance
Operations Management	
Organizational Behavior and Administration	
Managerial Policy and Strategy	

21 semester hours of upper-division coursework in the College of Business Administration. Among these must be 12 hours from the following:

Advanced Organizational Behaviour and Organizational Theory	Special Topics in Management
	Design of Productive System
	Collective Bargaining
Personnel Management	Personnel Assessment
Personnel Field Practice	
Advanced Operations Management	
Introduction to Operations Research	

Table 3: Average Semester Hours Taken in Selected Fields and Percentages of Those Hours Taken at Colleges Other Than the University

Fields	Physics Students (N = 17)	Management Students (N = 36)
Average total hours	157 (24.2%)	134 (29.1%)
Physics	48 (10.3%)	
Management		23 (09.5%)
English	9 (31.5%)	11 (47.1%)
Government	6 (33.3%)	7 (48.8%)
History	6 (39.5%)	8 (58.1%)
Math	30 (20.4%)	8 (62.5%)

Management students took over 45 per cent of all their liberal arts hours from other schools. Fourteen of the 36 whose transcripts were examined in detail took no history or government at the university, while only six of the 36 took all of their government and history courses at the university (by contrast, only four of the 17 physics students received their degrees without taking history or government courses at the university). Much the same was true of the introductory coursework (which, significantly, served to 'weed out' students who began their careers at the university). Only 54 per cent of the management students' courses in economics were taken at the university, 55 per cent of their courses in accounting, and 37.5 per cent of their math courses. Eleven of the 36 students in the random sample took no accounting courses at the university, 12 took no economics courses, and 19 took no math. By contrast, very few transfer credits were used in finance (7.8 per cent of total hours in finance), marketing (15.9 per cent) or business law (19.5 per cent).

Although the courses appear closely connected in disciplinary representations such as course requirements and transcripts, they occupied unconnected positions in the material organization of disciplinary space-time. Physics and management students could fulfill their 'English requirements', for example, at one of thousands of post-secondary institutions in the country, at two or more different institutions, or through tests that allowed them to 'place out' of the courses. This kind of spatial dispersion of courses outside the major made it less likely that they would be connected through network links or that students could relate them to one another in substantive ways. It almost certainly precluded a group effect on physics and management majors — whatever they took away from their scattered non-major courses was almost certainly different from what their co-majors took.

Concentration of Courses within the Major

If the courses outside the major were scattered through space-time, the opposite was true of courses in the major field. Only 31.7 per cent of the physics students' and 17.5 per cent of the management students' required coursework was in their major field (cf. Levine, 1978, pp. 31–4). However, the university I studied, like many others, required students seeking degrees to take most of the courses in the major 'in residence' on the university's campus. The result was that students took about 90 per cent of their coursework in the major field at the university (Table 3). Moreover, whereas the vast majority of general education courses could be taken in any order, courses in programs such as physics and management were temporally organized by prerequisite requirements. The physics and math courses were interlocked so that, in theory at least, from their first through their final semesters physics majors moved through a sequence of courses completely structured by prerequisites.

Management had a more complicated structure: a sequenced set of business courses required of all business majors, along with three sequenced management courses. Somewhere during the management students' third or fourth year of studies they also had to take four management courses (from a variable number of options) that were sequenced in different ways to the main set of courses. The resulting temporal organization created small clusters of sequenced courses rather than a single long string as in physics.

Official sequencing rules such as these exaggerate the pace at which courses were actually taken: college catalogs portray undergraduates marching through their courses of study in four years, eight full-time semesters. In the sample of transcripts I studied, only 21 per cent of the management graduates and only 5 per cent of the physics graduates matriculated in four years. About a quarter of the students in the two fields spent more than four years because they changed majors in mid-course; others transferred to the university from other schools and had to re-take courses. One major source of delay in physics was doing poorly in a course: 29 per cent of the graduates had flunked a physics course and had had to re-take it before continuing with the program.

The most common source of delay, however, was the strategic slowing of the official pace: students took 12 hours a semester rather than the expected 15. Management students took some of their courses in the summer to allow themselves these lighter course loads. Physics students would frequently register for a course, then drop it and re-take it in a later semester.

Although the pacing varies in this fashion, the official course sequences *do* define the general trajectory of students' paths through a program — a trajectory lacking in the non-major courses. The transcripts show that with few exceptions courses outside the major were not sequenced by prerequisites. They were temporally scattered across the students' academic careers (the general exception being the positioning of 'Freshman English' in the first or second semester of studies). Although the temporal fragmentation of non-major courses doesn't necessarily mean that they weren't organized into knowledge-constitutive networks, it does, along with the spatial dispersion mentioned earlier, make such network effects much less likely in courses outside the major. At least, this seemed to be the case for the students I interviewed.

In choosing non-major courses, for example, management students spoke of looking for four things: convenient hours, easiness (does the professor tell you exactly what he wants and then test you over it), entertaining teachers, and entertaining subject matter. Joe, for example, praised his class in the 'History of Motion Pictures' thus:

I took that because I heard it was real easy, taking it as an elective. And again, it was the same case, [the professor] was just incredible, one of the best, probably the best teacher I've had at [the university]. The tests were relatively easy. . . . He was just really clear on what you had to know.

By contrast, he spoke slightingly of courses like English:

The English, I guess it's probably important to have, to have a little knowledge of literature and the correct way to write — that's certainly important. But I felt like it was a little overemphasized. . . . I had, let's see, composition the first semester, and then your Masterworks of Literature — which I, I guess it's good to know stories by Thoreau and Poe and all those guys. But I don't feel it's necessary.

Similarly Curtis, who didn't like to read, spoke of having 'lucked out' in taking a literature class where the course work consisted of 'learn[ing] a bunch about the authors. Where they were born. What their parents did':

most of what we read wasn't that long. It wasn't like going home and reading 50 pages before class. It was more like maybe 15. Sometimes we'd read two or three poems that were like half a page each. As far as the reading part of that course, it wasn't that bad. It was more trying to figure out what they mean.

Physics students, by contrast, had far fewer non-major courses to take and could occasionally find classes relevant to the sciences that fulfilled their non-science requirements: a 'parageography' course in the humanities, history courses on the history of science, an archeo-astronomy course in anthropology, sociology courses on nuclear power and weaponry. On the whole, they looked more favourably on non-major courses than the management students, but still formulated their approval as appreciations of particular unrelated courses rather than connected sequences of courses:

Let's see, I did get something out of the government class I took. I had a very good professor who was very animated and it was on Civil Liberties under the Constitution . . . and he made it very interesting, and I came out knowing a lot more about Civil Liberties. Ah, the other government class I had it was really more just a grind, it was just the basic introduction to government, and I don't know that I hadn't had all of that stuff before. I took an anthropology class, the study of folklore, and I found that really interesting, really enjoyed it. . . . We studied more contemporary things as well as some of the older folklore. . . . Let me see, the English classes that I took, we covered some new material, I don't know that I got anything out of it except just the enjoyment of covering the material. I really didn't learn anything new . . . except maybe learned some new things about some stories (Bob).

As the quotations suggest, for both groups of students there were no patterned movements through the space outside the major, no transformations in social relations of mind, no connection among the contexts of the non-major courses.

The spatial localization and temporal sequencing of courses in the major marked them off from courses outside the major. If undergraduate education had systematic effects on students — if it produced 'outlooks', 'skills', 'knowledge', or 'ways of knowing' characteristic of groups — then these effects were produced *in the major*. The non-major courses may have stayed in memory, hardly registered, or been immediately forgotten — but in any event they were monuments glimpsed at a distance, not places lived in, not integral parts of the journey into the discipline.

Appendix 2

Making Knowledge About
Knowledge in Motion

What I planned when I started my fieldwork was over-ambitious. I was going to carry out an ethnography of four programs at a major university. I analyzed catalog requirements and enrolment statistics to select two 'academic' fields that seemed to have a graduate emphasis (physics and sociology), and two that seemed to have an 'applied' undergraduate emphasis (management and secondary science education). The programs were also selected to produce dimensions of some substantive comparison: physics and science education both dealing with 'science' issues, management and sociology with 'human social behaviour' issues.

I hoped that studying programs with such contrasting structures would allow me to say something about how curricula — the sequences of courses required for a degree — shaped student learning.

I began by approaching the Deans of the four colleges concerned to gain their permission for the study, then I met with department chairs to get their OKs. All were open to letting me approach faculty in their departments. My goal was to interview all faculty who'd taught undergraduate courses in the preceding year. This meant almost all of the sociology and secondary science education faculty, about half of the management professors, and a relatively small number of physics faculty. However, some teaching assignments were unfilled until just before the beginning of the semester (e.g., for the introductory courses in sociology and management) and in other cases teaching assignments were changed at fairly late dates (in physics and sociology). In addition to this, many faculty simply were not on campus or available before the beginning of the fall semester. For such reasons, the process of introducing myself to faculty and making arrangements to interview them continued into mid-October.

Finding and talking to the faculty I could identify wasn't all that easy. Many didn't post office hours, wouldn't return calls, and didn't show up when their secretaries expected. When I walked into sociology and physics office areas dressed in a suit I was taken as a textbook salesman, but if I ventured around the business school in anything less formal I was looked at askance as an uncouth student. As it turned out, most of the faculty, once I found them, were very gracious (the exceptions were physics faculty, some of whom were as curt to me as to their students). I tried to meet them first to get a copy of the syllabuses for their undergraduate courses, to set up an interview at a later date, and to get permission to observe classes.

Only one faculty member declined to be interviewed on tape, and even he was willing to speak informally. The interviews averaged about 30 minutes in length and focused mainly on three areas: (a) the instructors' views of the goals of the departments, the place of their courses in the department, and the characteristics of the department that influenced how they taught; (b) what their goals were for the courses in question, how they taught them, why they selected the particular texts they used, what kinds of students they had, how they evaluated students, and so forth; and (c) their own research interests, collegial ties, and status in the department. The questions about course goals and activities usually focused on statements and assignments on the syllabus. I had a list of questions which I used to remind myself of issues I wanted to talk about. I did not worry about preserving the exact wording of the questions or any particular order. Thus the interviews, especially the sections dealing with the syllabuses, were relatively unstructured. I did a total of 45 interviews with faculty (twelve in management, nine in physics, eighteen in sociology, and six in education).

I did attempt to compare the syllabuses I collected to those used in the same departments at other universities with similar national rankings. I bought catalogs from the colleges and wrote to department heads to try to arrange for them to send me copies of syllabuses, but the response was so uneven I had to abandon the effort.

Talking to Students

Getting access to students was easier in some ways, but 'sampling' the student body was harder. The adviser in the physics department helped me get names and phone numbers of physics students. The advisers at the business school, on the other hand, told me that although names of majors and phone numbers were public information, and thus legally accessible to me, students *could*, if they wished, make such information restricted. Well, I said, don't give me those. Ah, they replied, we don't know which ones might have made such a request, they're not flagged on the computer, so we can't give you any names lest one of the restricted ones slips through. In sociology and education there weren't even any advisers to approach. (To obtain lists of students in the four majors from the central office would require — so I was told — special programming and this in turn would cost money and require elaborate time-consuming delays and negotiations.)

In management, sociology and education, then, I simply concentrated on attending classes (courses that all majors in the program would be required to take, not electives), and (in management) student association meetings. I got to know and talk to students informally, and a few weeks into the semester I surveyed students in all of the classes I sat in on. The surveys included a written statement describing the project and were distributed with a sales pitch designed to interest students in being interviewed. Students who wanted to participate were asked to sign and provide a phone number at the bottom of the survey form. From both groups I'd try to recruit students for formal interviews. Again, the 'sample' isn't representative or random, the students are analysts whose perspectives are points of entry in the explication of their programs (Smith, 1987).

In selecting students for formal interviews I concentrated on seniors for a couple of reasons. First, I wanted to be able to talk with them about their academic careers in their programs. Second, I discovered that in management and sociology, at least, few students 'declared' the major before their senior year. In fact, the only program with sizeable enrolments at the freshman and sophomore level was physics, and there I did observe a sophomore class and interview second-year students. I interviewed eighteen sociology students, eighteen in secondary science education, fourteen in management, and eighteen in physics (eleven seniors, seven sophomores). This, of course, does not include the regular informal conversations that I had with students in each of the majors. The formal student interviews were, like the faculty interviews, loosely structured and open-ended, though I had a fairly elaborate set of questions. They averaged between 45 minutes and one hour in length.

Classroom Observations

The problem of how to examine what actually went on in the courses of the majors — how curriculum was enacted — was a difficult one. The common practice in research on college classrooms has been to use techniques and methods modelled on those developed for research on public school classrooms (e.g., Ellner and Barnes, 1983). The basic though usually unacknowledged assumption behind these approaches is that the classroom can be treated as a self-contained unit of activity that can be meaningfully analyzed in terms of what teacher behaviours seem connected to what student 'outcomes'. But of course students' interpretive strategies shape their responses to the demands or tasks of the teacher. Moreover, key activities such as note-taking, textbook reading, studying for tests, paper writing, homework problem-solving, and so forth, take place outside the classroom. The kinds of detailed observation notes that I was accustomed to taking in high school and junior high classrooms (verbatim accounts of speech, running sometimes to almost 40 pages long for a 50 minute class) were of limited use in studying the lectures and presentations that characterize most classrooms at the university (or for that matter, discussions in the occasional seminar classes).

I made close observations of some 100-odd class sessions, in addition to regular observations of student problem-solving sessions (especially common in physics), and of student study outside the classroom (e.g., group work in case analysis in business). This was in addition to my daily note-taking and

observation of students in libraries, campus meeting places, student associations, and so forth.

Transcript Analysis

I analyzed copies of 225 transcripts representing all of the students who'd
graduated with degrees in the four fields over the most recent year for which
records were available (getting access to these records — even with the names
removed — took about six months of negotiation). The analysis focused on
the number of issues: the number of hours taken and semesters attended, the
number of hours taken in the major field and outside it, the number of hours
transferred from other institutions, grades made in and outside the major, the
kinds of electives taken by students in the different majors and the sequence
and timing in which they were taken, and so forth.

What Happened to Sociology and Secondary Science Education?

The book deals with physics and management alone. There were some prag-
matic reasons for this exclusion (length being an obvious one) but the basic
problem with incorporating sociology and secondary science education into
the account is that they're different kinds of educational experiences, different
kinds of stories. Physics and management were programs that seemed to
generate group effects by moving students through shared material and representational organizations of space-time. Sociology and secondary science
education were spread out across the campus, had no regular temporal organization, and no group effects.

As I had initially surmised, graduate education was the main focus of
teaching in sociology. I had assumed, however, that as in my own experience
in anthropology, the undergraduate program performed the role of socializing
and recruiting students into a graduate school orientation in their field. This
was not the case. As a professor explained, the goal of the department was:

> Training graduate students who will then make a name for themselves
> which will build up the reputation of the department here and benefit
> everybody who's in it. It's not to teach undergraduates.

The last sentence in this statement must be qualified slightly: if it was not
important to teach undergraduates sociology, it was important to have a lot of
students in undergraduate sociology courses. First, to enter the graduate program in sociology at this, as at many universities, one did not need an undergraduate degree in sociology. Thus the undergraduate program did not function
as a recruiting ground for the graduate program, as was the case in physics.
Second, sociology was funding-poor relative to the sciences and the business

school, meaning that it could not rely on outside funding as the principal support for its graduate program. Third, the rules and 'course load formulas' regulating teaching assignments and the allocation of teaching assistantships made large courses desirable in sociology. Without going into details, the formulas created a situation in which the larger the courses a professor taught, the fewer courses he or she had to teach, and the greater the number of graduate teaching assistantships allotted to the department. These assistantships supported the graduate program in the absence of large and steady sources of outside funding.

These factors created pressures for courses that attracted large enrolments and worked against a sequencing of courses structured by prerequisites. Aside from the four completely determined courses required of majors, the majority of sociology course offerings dealt with topical, high-interest issues (e.g., nuclear war) or areas of perennial interest (e.g., sex roles). As one professor explained, 'marketing' was 'part of the logic' for such curricular decisions:

> If you have under 'social problems' a course on say, racism, sexism, violence, any number of things, chances are you're going to attract more people overall than if you have one or two sections on 'social problems' in general.

It would be misleading to say that these courses were offered because they attracted large enrolments. The courses represented areas of genuine concern to the faculty who taught them — but it was the need for enrolments that created the opening for faculty to pursue these concerns. Thus sociology faculty had given little thought to the undergraduate curriculum beyond their own courses, as can be seen in the following exchange:

> [*Nespor*: There are four required courses in the undergraduate curriculum . . . Why four, why those four?]
> A sacred sociological number [laughs]. . . . Well it seems to me like, ah, let me say I have not done a lot of conscious reflection on the undergraduate sociology curriculum. . . . I suppose part of it is career trajectory. That's something that I've been able to avoid, and I have to avoid a lot of things in order to make it in the academic world.

While atomizing the courses and denying any necessary connection among them (let alone a cumulative effect on students), the curricular structure was a marketing device, a way of generating undergraduate enrolments to help support the graduate program. Students majoring in sociology, for their part, used the commodity being marketed to their own ends: obtaining a degree.

Undergraduate sociology wasn't really a 'program'. It was a set of loose requirements (21 hours in sociology, without prerequisite requirements) that attracted students who'd left other programs. In the transcript analysis, for example, I found that 37 per cent of the students who'd graduated with BAs in sociology had entered the program after flunking out of the business school. Undergraduate sociology courses were not organized into a sequence or network tied together in a material organization of space-time. Instead, they were constructed to attact large numbers of students, which in turn generated assistantships for graduate students and reduced the teaching loads of the faculty. It was the graduate program (which rated in the top twenty nationally, see Jones, Lindzey and Coggeshall, 1982) that faculty were concerned about. The undergraduate courses were cash-cows supporting it. Only one of the eighteen students 'majoring' in sociology I interviewed was thinking of continuing to graduate school in the field. The others were going into the workforce upon graduation and had ended up in sociology because it had the lowest number of requirements and it allowed them to get a degree in *some* area rather than leaving school without a degree.

Like sociology, secondary science education didn't function as a 'program' in the way management and physics did. Secondary science education faculty intended their program to prepare students for the workplace, teaching specific fields of science at the secondary level. The science education program was distinctive, however, in its dependence on other departments and colleges of the university — in particular those in the natural sciences. First, the major drew its students from these fields: students who had initially intended to major in a science or engineering field, and had later decided to teach. The science departments also decided what kind of science courses students should take, and taught the courses as well. As a result, there was a lot of variability across disciplines. At one extreme, secondary science students getting certified in biology had to take 26 total hours in biology (in courses of their choice), while at the other extreme, students getting certified in chemistry had to take 29 hours in chemistry (all of them specified by the chemistry department and 23 of them sequenced by prerequisites) and six additional hours in science. Not surprisingly, 16 of the 31 recent graduates whose transcripts I examined had biology as their main concentration while only one specialized in chemistry.

Lacking control over their students' science curricula, the education faculty generally expressed dissatisfaction with it. As one secondary science education faculty member explained:

> I typically give them [the students] a pre-test when we first start, to find out what their understanding of fundamental concepts or basic concepts is. For instance, this semester not one of those students, even though they got over 3.0 average in their science courses, with almost 60 semester hours in science, not one of them could define molecule in an accurate way. Not one could operationally define temperature. It was a very small per cent that could define volume. None of them — I shouldn't say none — but it's rare that any of them have any notion at all about the nature of science, in terms of the nature of scientific laws or theories or how they are evolved. They've had practically no preparation in terms of any kinds of thinking skills like

drawing inferences from data and the processes involved. Our science courses at the university level just don't do anything for them, at least not those kinds of things. . . . They really do need a different kind of science than what they're getting, because the kind of science they're getting isn't helping them to teach kids at all.

One faculty explanation for this was that 'teacher preparation is not one of their priorities in the natural sciences.' Another explanation, however, emerges from the transcript analysis of 31 students who graduated over a three semester period. The transcripts show that most of the science courses students took were introductory science courses. By 'introductory' I mean a course that actually serves as the first in the major (has the lowest course number, requires no prerequisites) or a lower-division course that requires no prerequisites and is designed for the general, non-science student (e.g., 'Botany for Gardeners'). Using this definition, 84 per cent of the physical science coursework of students concentrating in physical science was introductory, 40 per cent of the biology coursework of students concentrating in biology was introductory, and 41 per cent of the earth science coursework of students getting science specializations was introductory.

What these numbers suggest, and as was borne out in interviews with students, the curriculum merely set numerical levels of course taking to define acceptable exposure to a field. Students selectively sampled from the fields in order to acccumulate the needed hours in the easiest manner possible. They did not participate in the student cultures of the science fields nor did they construct images of the fields as intellectual domains: by focusing mainly on introductory and lower-level courses (designed by the science faculty either as enrolment generators or as 'weed-out' courses, and in both cases organized around the routinized presentation of material and 'objective' test formats such as multiple-choice) the students came to look at the sciences as disjointed aggregations of 'facts' (something the students resented: they referred to their science courses as 'scarf and barf' courses and complained of their uselessness).

Although the courses in the education portion of the secondary science education curriculum were sequenced by prerequisites, there were no substantive connections across them. In part this was because the curriculum had been buffeted by legislative interventions in the certification standards for school teachers. New courses were created while other portions of the curriculum were truncated. The courses that were recent, state-mandated additions to the curriculum were not well-integrated with the other education courses. One, for example, tried to address such topics as 'the organization of schools', 'legal aspects of schooling', 'ethical aspects of schooling', 'attention to students with varying needs', and 'media'. It was, as one faculty member explained, 'a combination of various topics put into one three-hour course, and they don't necessarily fit together in any meaningful way.' Even the more established courses of the curriculum, such as educational psychology were, in the words of one instructor, 'discontinuous' with the rest of the preparation program.

The shared programmatic experiences of the secondary science students, then, really amounted to two courses (Secondary School Teaching and Secondary Science Methods) and student teaching — not really a 'program' in the sense I've been using in this book. Thus, as I've suggested earlier in this book and elsewhere (Nespor, 1990b) physics and management reflected kinds of disciplinary educations — the movement of students into networks of power — not post-secondary education generally. Each student graduating from sociology and secondary science education had a unique rather than a shared trajectory through the space-time of the university: the stories of those students are important stories, but they're not the ones I'm telling here.

Making Knowledge about Knowledge in Motion

I cannot conclude without acknowledging the tension between the theoretical ambitions of this book and the practices of research and writing that created it.

Consider the interview material I draw upon in the book. Standard interviewing practice focuses discussion on the researcher's topics and, insofar as those topics are drawn from the academic literature, transforms the interviewee into a commentator on the categories of the disciplinary discourse (Smith, 1977). But interviews do more than shape content. First, they 'foreshorten time' (Rose, 1987, p. 24). Instead of experiencing the rhythm and improvisatory nature of an event we are provided with a map of it as already completed (Bourdieu, 1977). Second, interviews reify the 'individual' as a source of knowledge. We hear accounts constructed from the perspective of a single, seemingly independent source (ignoring our own role as interlocutor). Third, interviews produce accounts that are 'referential' (unambiguously indicating people or things in the 'real world') and devoid of tone or expressive or creative features (Briggs, 1986, pp. 116–19). In short, as Briggs (1986) argues, interviewing produces an 'initial decontextualization of the data even before we begin the analysis' (p. 118). 'Coding' and the other standard components of interview analysis further decontextualize speech until its spatial and temporal groundings are no longer visible:

> Standard sociological analysis uses some method of coding and interpreting such accounts to order the interview materials in relation to the relevances of the sociological . . . discourses. These enable the interviews to be sorted into topics typical of the study population. In such a process, the standpoint of the women [or men] themselves is suppressed. The standpoint becomes that of the discourse reflecting upon properties of the study population. Characteristics of the study population become the object of the knower's gaze (Smith, p. 182).

Our methodologies decontextualize practice to produce 'data': they suppress its temporal and spatial organization and ignore the space-time organization of the researcher's practice that produces the analytic account (my preoccupation with academic work is just one example of what Smith calls the 'sectioning out' of experience by research practices). Our practices of representation produce the object of knowledge as a spatially bounded and self-contained entity, either static or unfolding regularly through time.

I do not pretend to have overcome these difficulties. My interviews, for example, tended to suppress the expressive and poetic features of discourse. My questions focused primarily on the work of schooling: choosing majors, selecting courses, doing assignments, and so forth. They didn't allow students to construct themselves as, say, 'emotional' selves. My observations were of academic events and social activities on the university campus and don't even touch upon life off campus, at work, during the summers, and so forth.

The book, then, is a very partial story. The basic strategy that underlies its construction flows from Rosaldo's (1989) suggestion that the accounts of people be treated not as 'data' to be 'analyzed' in terms of a disciplinary discourse, but as informed analyses in their own right (Rosaldo, 1989, p. 142; cf. Gwaltney, 1980).

Treating interview discourse as 'analysis' means thinking of it as a situated account in which the speaker creates the 'objects' discussed in interaction with the interviewer. Narratives are a representational technology (Nespor and Barylske, 1991) that speakers use to constitute and explicate phenomena in the interview context, not referential accounts that can be 'coded' or reduced to categories that allow one speaker to be combined with others. In essence, I gave up some of the mobility, stability, and combinability of the interview discourse by reproducing it in lengthy, relatively immobile chunks that are unstable (in the sense that they allow alternative explications), and mix poorly because they are uncoded.

The book is not about students or student life, but curriculum and the organization of disciplinary knowledge in undergraduate education. The students were co-analysts, not objects of analysis, in the sense that while the text is ultimately my doing, the words and voices inscribed here are not entirely my own. There's a difference between weaving and quilting. I could not follow students across the four (or more) years of their studies, or duplicate their journeys, but I could draw on *their* accounts of these things. As Clifford (1988) points out, this is not a straightforward solution: using lengthy quotations accomplishes little if 'quotations are always staged by the quoter and tend merely to serve as examples or confirming testimony' (p. 51). My goal has been to make the quotations carry the burden of explication. But treating students' comments as analyses means reconciling ourselves to a text that doesn't 'resolve' into parsimonious explanations or interpretations. As Rosaldo (1989) suggests:

> Narrative analyses told or written from divergent perspectives . . . will not fit together into a unified master summation. . . . Social analysis thus becomes a relational form of understanding in which both parties actively engage in 'the interpretation of cultures'. Rather than being

perspectival, inscribed from within a single point of view, such forms of human understanding involve the irreducible perceptions of both analysts and their subjects. Much as two narratives usually do not map neatly onto one another, one party's analysis can only rarely be reduced to the terms of the other (pp. 147–8; 206–20).

This non-reductionist approach goes against the expectation — not just our own, but that of publishers, journal editors and most readers — that the multiple perspectives explored in a work will in the conclusion be reduced to one single account: that the author will explain 'what it all means'. Such expectations, again, are grounded in the spatio-temporal practices of social research that seek to inscribe, reduce, and mobilize the world in interpretations and explanations that allow actors at the center of a cycle of accumulation to speak for those elements of the world. As Smith (1987) puts it:

> The multiple perspectives of subjects, the multiple possible versions of the world arising in subjects' experience, create a problem for sociology only when our project is to establish a sociological version superseding theirs. It is a difficulty that arises largely from grounding sociology in 'meaning', 'interpretation', 'common understandings' and the like rather than in an ongoing coordering of actual activities accomplished in definite historical settings (p. 141).

As much as I resist it, I'm a creature of this way of reducing the world, as are all of us who write books. The best I can do with this text is try to position myself not as a translator of the people I studied, but as someone who traces and explicates the material and representational productions of space and time that link people to other people and things beyond their arenas of face-to-face interaction. My arguments do not subsume those of others. Rather, I've tried to situate their analyses, not interpret or explain them.

Aside from an unevenness in tone, which I've tried to minimize, this use of the students' comments may invite the complaint that the book is over-reliant on students' 'naive' accounts of their experience. But 'naivete,' like 'irrationality', is less a thing than an accusation (Latour, 1987). It seems to me absurd to suggest that I know more about being a physics student than the students do. My knowledge is no less 'local' than theirs: we simply build our networks of different shapes with different materials. They build their accounts through ongoing participation in the programs, I build my accounts in part out of their accounts. But this does not make my ideas more 'general' in some sense:

> No kind of work is *more* local than any other unless it has been conquered . . . and forced to yield a trace. Then it can be worked on *in its absence.* An African hunter who covers dozens of square miles and who has learned to recognize *hundreds of thousands* of signs and

marks is called a 'local'. But a cartographer who has learned to re-
cognize a *few hundred* signs and indices while leaning over a few
square yards of maps and aerial photographs is said to be more universal than the hunter and to have a global vision. Which one would
be more lost in the territory of the other? Unless we follow the long
history that has turned the hunter into a slave and the mapmaker into
a master, we can have no answer to this question. There is no pathway between the local and the global because there *is* no global
(Latour, 1988, pp. 219–20).

No 'global', no unifying narrative or perspective. What we're left with is
pathways and networks, and the task of figuring out how people get started
down a particular route and what happens to them as they traverse it.

References

AIP (American Institute of Physics) (1985) *Graduate Programs in Physics, Astronomy, and Related Fields*, New York: American Institute of Physics.

AIP (American Institute of Physics) (1988a) *Physics in the High Schools: Findings from the 1986–87 Nationwide Survey of Secondary School Teachers in Physics*, New York: American Institute of Physics.

AIP (American Institute of Physics) (1988b) *1986–87 Survey of Physics and Astronomy Bachelor's Degree Recipients*, New York: American Institute of Physics.

BATESON, G. (1972) 'Form, substance, and difference', in *Steps to an Ecology of Mind*, New York: Ballantine Books, pp. 448–65.

BEASLEY, M. and JONES, L. (1986) 'Education for research', *Physics Today*, **39**(6), pp. 36–44.

BERGER, J. (1974) *The Look of Things*, New York: Viking.

BERHMAN, J. and LEVIN, R. (1984) 'Are business schools doing their job?' *Harvard Business Review*, **62**, pp. 140–7.

BORDO, S. (1990) 'The body and the reproduction of femininity: A feminist appropriation of Foucault', in JAGGAR, A. and BORDO, S. (Eds) *Gender/Body/Knowledge: Feminist Reconstructions of Being and Knowing*, New Brunswick: Rutgers.

BOURDIEU, P. (1977) *Outline of a Theory of Practice*, Cambridge: Cambridge University Press.

BOURDIEU, P. (1986) 'The Forms of Capital', in RICHARDSON, J. (Ed.) *Handbook of Theory and Research for the Sociology of Education*, New York: Greenwood Press, pp. 241–58.

BOURDIEU, P. and BOLTANSKI, L. (1978) 'Changes in social structure and changes in the demand for education', in GINER, S. and ARCHER, M. (Eds) *Contemporary Europe: Social Structures and Cultural Processes*, London: Routledge & Kegan Paul, pp. 197–226.

BRIGGS, C. (1986) *Learning How to Ask*, Cambridge: Cambridge University Press.

BROOKS, H. (1978) 'The dynamics of funding, enrolments, curriculum and employment', in PERL, M. (Ed.) *Physics Careers, Employment and Education*, New York: American Institute of Physics, pp. 94–108.

BUCKLEY, M. and EDER, R. (1988) 'B.M. Springbett and the notion of the "snap decision" in the interview', *Journal of Management*, **14** (March), pp. 59–67.

BURAWOY, M. (1979) *Manufacturing Consent*, Chicago: University of Chicago Press.

BUTLER, J. (1990) *Gender Trouble: Feminism and the Subversion of Identity*, New York: Routledge.

CALLON, M. (1986) 'Some elements of a sociology of translation: Domestication of the scallops and the fishermen', in LAW, J. (Ed.) *Power, Action and Belief: A New Sociology of Knowledge?* Sociological Review Monograph, No. 32 (University of Keele), London: Routledge and Kegan Paul, pp. 196–229.

CALLON, M. (1987) 'Society in the making: The study of technology as a tool for sociological analysis', in BIJKER, W., HUGHES, T. and PINCH, T. (Eds) *The Social Construction of Technological Systems*, Cambridge, MA: The MIT Press, pp. 83–103.

CALLON, M. and LATOUR, B. (1981) 'Unscrewing the big Leviathan, or how actors macrostructure reality and how sociologists help them do so', in KNORR-CETINA, K. and CICOUREL, A. (Eds) *Advances in Social Theory and Methodology: Towards an Integration of Micro and Macro Sociologies*, London: Routledge and Kegan Paul.

CHANDLER, A. (1977) *The Visible Hand: The Managerial Revolution in American Business*, Cambridge, MA: Belknap Press.

CLEGG, S. (1990) *Frameworks of Power*, London: Sage.

CLIFFORD, J. (1988) 'On ethnographic authority', in *The Predicament of Culture*, Cambridge, MA: Harvard University Press, pp. 21–54.

COLLINS, R. (1979) *The Credential Society*, New York: Academic Press.

COSER, L., KADUSHIN, C. and POWELL, W. (1982) *Books: The Culture and Commerce of Publishing*, New York: Basic Books.

COULTER, J. (1983) *Rethinking Cognitive Theory*, London: Macmillan.

COX, A. (1986) *Inside Corporate America*, New York: St Martin's Press.

CRAWFORD, F. (1968) *Waves, Berkeley Physics Course, Vol. 3*, New York: McGraw-Hill.

CULLER, J. (1983) *On Deconstruction: Theory and Criticism after Structuralism*, London: Routledge.

DALTON, M. (1959) *Men Who Manage*, New York: John Wiley and Sons.

DE CERTEAU, M. (1984) *The Practice of Everyday Life*, Berkeley: University of California Press.

DIMAGGIO, P. and POWELL, W. (1983) 'The iron cage revisited: Institutional isomorphism and collective rationality in organizational fields', *American Sociological Review*, **48**, pp. 147–60.

EDER, D. (1990) 'Serious and playful disputes: Variation in conflict talk among female adolescents', in GRIMSHAW, A. (Ed.) *Conflict Talk: Sociolinguistic Investigations of Arguments in Conversations*, Cambridge: Cambridge University Press, pp. 67–84.

EISENHART, M. (1985) 'Women choose their careers: A study of natural decision making', *The Review of Higher Education*, **8**, pp. 247–70.

ELLNER, C. and BARNES, C. (1983) *Studies of College Teaching: Experimental*

Results, Theoretical Interpretations, and New Perspectives, Lexington, MA: Lexington Books.

ENGESTROM, Y. (1987) *Learning by Expanding: An Activity-Theoretical Approach to Developmental Research*, Helsinki: Orienta-Konsultit Oy.

ENTWISTLE, N. and RAMSDEN, P. (1982) *Understanding Student Learning*, London: Croom Helm.

ESTES, W.K. (1989) 'Learning theory', in LESGOLD, A. and GLASER, R. (Eds) *Foundations for a Psychology of Education*, Hillsdale, NJ: Lawrence Erlbaum, pp. 1–49.

FEYNMAN, R. (1965) *The Character of Physical Law*, Cambridge, MA: The MIT Press.

FOLEY, D. (1990) *Learning Capitalist Culture*, Philadelphia, PA: University of Pennsylvania Press.

FORSYTHE, S., DRAKE, M. and COX, C. (1985) 'Influence of applicant's dress on interviewer's selection decisions', *Journal of Applied Psychology*, **70**, pp. 586–601.

FOUCAULT, M. (1972) *The Archeology of Knowledge and the Discourse on Language*, New York: Random House.

FOUCAULT, M. (1979) *Discipline and Punish* (Trans. Alan Sheriden), New York: Vintage Books.

GIDDENS, A. (1979) *Central Problems in Social Theory: Action, Structure and Contradiction in Social Analysis*, Berkeley: University of California Press.

GIDDENS, A. (1981) *A Contemporary Critique of Historical Materialism, Vol. 1: Power, Property and the State*, Berkeley: University of California Press.

GIDDENS, A. (1985) 'Time, space and regionalisation', in GREGORY, D. and URRY, J. (Eds) *Social Relations and Spatial Relations*, New York: St Martin's Press, pp. 265–95.

GILLIGAN, C. (1982) *In a Different Voice: Psychological Theory and Women's Development*, Cambridge, MA: Harvard University Press.

GOFFMAN, E. (1971) *Relations in Public*, New York: Harper.

GOODWIN, M.H. (1988) 'Cooperation and competition across girls' play activities', in TODD, A. and FISHER, S. (Eds) *Gender and Discourse: The Power of Talk*, Norwood, NJ: Ablex, pp. 55–94.

GORDON, R. and HOWELL, J. (1959) *Higher Education for American Business*, New York: Columbia University Press.

GRANOVETTER, M. (1983) 'The Strength of Weak Ties: A Network Theory Revisited', in COLLINS, R. (Ed.) *Sociological Theory, 1983*, San Francisco: Jossey-Bass, pp. 201–33.

GREENBLATT, S. (1981) 'Preface' in *Allegory and Representation*, Baltimore: Johns Hopkins University Press.

GREGORY, D. (1988) 'Areal differentiation and post-modern human geography', in GREGORY, D. and WALFORD, R. (Eds) *Horizons in Human Geography*, Totowa, NJ: Barnes & Noble, pp. 67–96.

GREGORY, D. (1994) *Geographical Imaginations*, London: Basil Blackwell.

GUPTA, A. and FERGUSON, J. (1992) 'Beyond "culture": Space, identity, and the politics of difference', *Cultural Anthropology*, **7**(1), pp. 6–23.

GWALTNEY, J.L. (1980) *Drylongso: A Self-Portrait of Black America*, New York: Vintage Books.

HACKER, S. (1989) *Pleasure, Power and Technology: Some Tales of Gender, Engineering, and the Cooperative Workplace*, Boston: Unwin Hyman.

HACKER, S. (1990) *'Doing it the Hard Way': Investigations of Gender and Technology*, Boston: Unwin and Hyman.

HALL, S. (1992) 'Cultural studies and its theoretical legacies', in GROSSBERG, L., NELSON, C. and TREICHLER, P. (Eds) *Cultural Studies*, New York: Routledge, pp. 277–86.

HARAWAY, D. (1988) 'Situated knowledges: The science question in feminism and the privilege of partial perspectives', *Feminist Studies*, **14**(3), pp. 575–99.

HARAWAY, D. (1989) *Primate Visions*, London: Routledge.

HARAWAY, D. (1991) 'The politics of postmodern bodies: Constitutions of self in immune system discourse', in *Simians, Cyborgs, and Women: The Reinvention of Nature*, New York: Routledge, pp. 203–30.

HARAWAY, D. (1992) 'The promise of monsters: A regenerative politics for inappropriat/d others', in GROSSBERG, L., NELSON, C. and TREICHLER, P. (Eds) *Cultural Studies*, New York: Routledge, pp. 295–337.

HARVEY, D. (1989) *The Condition of Post-Modernity*, Cambridge, MA: Basil Blackwell.

HEAD, J. (1985) *The Personal Response to Science*, Cambridge: Cambridge University Press.

HEARN, J. and OLZAK, S. (1981) 'The role of college major departments in the reproduction of sexual inequality', *Sociology of Education*, **54**, pp. 195–205.

HEILMAN, M. and SARUWATI, L. (1979) 'When beauty is beastly: The effects of appearance and sex on evaluations of job applicants for managerial and nonmanagerial jobs', *Organizational Behavior and Human Performance*, **23**, pp. 360–72.

HUGSTAD, P. (1983) *The Business School in the 1980s: Liberalism vs. Vocationalism*, New York: Praeger.

HURTADO, S. (1989, March) 'Inheriting a Career: Factors Influencing College Student Choice of a Parent's Career', paper presented at the Annual Meeting of the American Education Research Association, San Francisco, CA.

INTERNATIONAL UNION OF PURE AND APPLIED PHYSICS (1966) *A Survey of the Teaching of Physics at Universities*, Paris: UNESCO.

ISENBERG, D. (1987) 'Inside the mind of the senior manager', in PERKINS, D., LOCHHEAD, J. and BISHOP, J. (Eds) *Thinking: The Second International Conference*, Hillsdale, NJ: Lawrence Erlbaum, pp. 173–96.

JACKALL, R. (1988) *Moral Mazes: The World of Corporate Managers*, New York: Oxford University Press.

JAMESON, F. (1988) 'Cognitive mapping', in NELSON, C. and GROSSBERG, L. (Eds) *Marxism and the Interpretation of Culture*, Urbana, IL: University of Illinois Press, pp. 347–57.

JONES, L., LINDZEY, G. and COGGESHALL, P. (1982) *An Assessment of Research-Doctorate Programs in the United States*, Washington, DC: National Academy Press.

JONES, T. (1986) 'Liberal learning and undergraduate business study', in JOHNSTON, J.S. Jr. *et al. Educating Managers*, San Francisco: Jossey-Bass, pp. 124–42.

KANTER, R.M. (1977) *Men and Women of the Corporation*, New York: Basic Books.

KATCHADOURIAN, H. and BOLI, J. (1985) *Careerism and Intellectualism Among College Students*, San Francisco: Jossey-Bass.

KEVLES, D. (1978) *The Physicists: The History of a Scientific Community in Modern America*, New York: Alfred Knopf.

KLEPPNER, D. (1985) 'Research in small groups', *Physics Today*, **38**(3), pp. 79–85.

KONDO, D. (1990) *Crafting Selves*, Chicago: University of Chicago Press.

KUHN, T. (1963) 'The function of measurement in modern science', in *Quantification: A History of the Meaning of Measurement in the Natural and Social Science*, Indianapolis, IN: The Bobbs-Merrill Co., pp. 31–63.

KUHN, T. (1970) *The Structure of Scientific Revolutions, Second Edition*, Chicago: The University of Chicago Press.

KVALE, S. (1983) 'The quantification of knowledge in education: On resistance toward qualitative evaluation and research', in BAIN, B. (Ed.) *The Sociogenesis of Language and Cognition*, New York: Plenum Press, pp. 433–47.

LCHC (Laboratory of Comparative Human Cognition) (1982) 'Culture and intelligence', in STERNBERG, R. (Ed.) *Handbook of Human Intelligence*, New York: Cambridge University Press, pp. 642–719.

LCHC (Laboratory of Comparative Human Cognition) (1983) 'Culture and cognitive development', in MUSSEN, P. (Ed.) *Handbook of Child Psychology, Vol. 1*, New York: John Wiley & Sons, pp. 295–356.

LARKIN, J. (1985) 'Understanding, problem representations, and skill in physics', CHIPMAN, S., SEGAL, J. and GLASER, R. (Eds) *Thinking and Learning Skills, Vol. 2, Research and Open Questions*, Hillsdale, NJ: Lawrence Erlbaum, pp. 141–59.

LATOUR (1986a) 'Visualization and cognition: Thinking with eyes and hands', *Knowledge and Society: Studies in the Sociology of Culture Past and Present*, **6**, pp. 1–40.

LATOUR, B. (1986b) 'The powers of association', in LAW, J. (Ed.) *Power, Action and Belief: A New Sociology of Knowledge?*, Sociological Review Monograph No. 32 (University of Keele), London: Routledge & Kegan Paul, pp. 264–80.

LATOUR, B. (1987) *Science in Action*, Cambridge, MA: Harvard University Press.

LATOUR, B. (1988) *The Pasteurization of France*, Cambridge, MA: Harvard University Press.

LATOUR, B. (1989) 'The politics of explanation', in WOOLGAR, S. (Ed.) *Knowledge and Reflexivity*, London: Sage, pp. 155–76.

LATOUR, B. (1990) 'Drawing things together', in LYNCH, M. and WOOLGAR, S. (Eds) *Representation in Scientific Practice*, Cambridge, MA: The MIT Press, pp. 19–68.

LATOUR, B. and WOOLGAR, S. (1986) *Laboratory Life: The Construction of Scientific Facts*, Princeton: Princeton University Press.

LAVE, J. (1988) *Cognition in Practice: Mind, Mathematics and Culture in Everyday Life*, New York: Cambridge University Press.

LAVE, J. and WENGER, E. (1991) *Situated Learning: Legitimate Peripheral Performance*, Cambridge: Cambridge University Press.

LAVIE, S. (1990) *The Poetics of Military Occupation*, Berkeley: University of California Press.

LEFEBVRE, H. (1991) *The Production of Space* (Translated by Donald Nicholson-Smith), Oxford, UK: Blackwell.

LESGOLD, A. (1988) 'Problem-solving', in STERNBERG, R. and SMITH, E. (Eds) *The Psychology of Human Thought*, Cambridge: Cambridge University Press, pp. 188–213.

LEVER, J. (1976) 'Sex differences in the games children play', *Social Problems*, **23**, pp. 478–87.

LEVINE, A. (1978) *Handbook on Undergraduate Curriculum*, San Francisco: Jossey-Bass.

LYNCH, M. (1988) 'The externalized retina: Selection and mathematization in the visual documentation of objects in the life sciences', in LYNCH, M. and WOOLGAR, S. (Eds) *Representation in Scientific Practice*, Cambridge, MA: The MIT Press, pp. 153–86.

MCDERMOTT, L. (1990) 'A view from physics', in GARDNER, M., GREENO, J., REIF, F., SCHOENFELD, A., DISESSA, A. and STAGE, E. (Eds) *Toward a Scientific Practice of Science Education*, Hillsdale, NJ: Lawrence Erlbaum, pp. 3–30.

MANDT, E. (1982) 'The failure of business education — and what to do about it', *Management Review*, **71**(8), pp. 47–52.

MARCEAU, J. (1979) 'Business policies, business elites and business schools', *Social Science Information*, **13**, pp. 473–86.

MARCH, J. and SIMON, H. (1958) *Organizations*, New York: John Wiley & Sons.

MARCUS, G. (1991) 'A broad(er)side to the Canon being a partial account of a year of travel among textual communities in the realm of humanities centers and including a collection of artificial curiosities', *Cultural Anthropology*, **6**(1), pp. 385–405.

MARTON, F. (1984) 'Towards a psychology beyond the individual', in LAGERSPETZ, K. and NIEMI, P. (Eds) *Psychology in the 1990s*, North-Holland: Elsevier Science Publishers, pp. 45–72.

MARTON, F. and SVENSSON, L. (1979) 'Conceptions of research in student learning', *Higher Education*, **8**, pp. 471–86.

MARX, K. (1967) *Capital, Vol. 1*, New York: International Publishers.

MASSEY, D. (1993) 'Power-geometry and a progressive sense of place', in BIRD, J., CURTIS, B., PUTNAM, T., ROBERTSON, G. and TUCKER, L. (Eds) *Mapping the Futures: Local Cultures, Global Change*, London: Routledge.

MEMORY, J., ARNOLD, J., STEWART, D. and FORNES, R. (1985) 'Physics as a team sport', *American Journal of Physics*, **53**(3), pp. 270–1.

MOERMAN, M. (1989) *Talking Culture: Ethnography and Conversation Analysis*, Philadelphia, PA: University of Pennsylvania Press.

MOLL, L. (Ed.) (1991) *Vygotsky and Education*, Cambridge: Cambridge University Press.

MOTOWIDLO, S. (1986) 'Information processing in personnel decisions', *Research in Personnel and Human Resources Management*, **4**, Greenwood, CT: JAI Press, pp. 1–44.

NESPOR, J. (1990a) 'The Jackhammer: A case study of undergraduate physics problem-solving in its social setting', *International Journal of Qualitative Studies in Education* **3**(2), pp. 139–55.

NESPOR, J. (1990b) 'Curriculum and conversions of capital in the acquisition of disciplinary knowledge', *Journal of Curriculum Studies*, **22**, pp. 217–32.

NESPOR, J. (1990c) 'Grades and knowledge in higher education', *Journal of Curriculum Studies*, **22**(6), pp. 545–56.

NESPOR, J. and BARYLSKE, J. (1991) 'Narrative discourse and teacher knowledge', *American Educational Research Journal*, **28**, pp. 805–23.

NEWMAN, D. (1990) 'Using social context for science teaching', in GARDNER, M., GREENO, J., REIF, F., SCHOENFELD, A., DISESSA, A. and STAGE, E. (Eds) *Toward a Scientific Practice of Science Education*, Hillsdale, NJ: Lawrence Erlbaum, pp. 187–202.

NEWMAN, D. GRIFFIN, P. and COLE, M. (1989) *The Construction Zone: Working for Cognitive Change in Schools*, Cambridge: Cambridge University Press.

NYRE, G. and REILLY, K. (1979) *Professional Education in the Eighties: Challenges and Responses*, AAHE/ERIC Research Report No. 8, Washington, DC: American Association for Higher Education.

OHANIAN, H. (1985) *Physics, Vol. 1*, New York: W.W. Norton.

OLSON, D. (1980) 'On the language and authority of textbooks', *Journal of Communication*, **30**, pp. 186–98.

ORTH, C. (1963) *Social Structure and Learning Climate: The First Year at the Harvard Business School*, Boston, MA: Division of Research, Graduate School of Business Administration, Harvard University.

PALLRAND, G. and LINDENFELD, P. (1985) 'The physics classroom revisited: Have we learned our lesson?', *Physics Today*, **38**(11), pp. 46–52.

PASK, G. (1976) 'Styles and strategies of learning', *British Journal of Educational Psychology*, **46**, pp. 128–48.

PERRUCCI, R. and POTTER, H. (Eds) (1989) *Networks of Power: Organizational Actors at the National, Corporate, and Community Levels*, New York: Aldine de Gruyter.

PERRY, W.G. (1970) *Forms of Intellectual and Ethical Development in the College Years: A Scheme*, New York: Holt, Rinehart & Winston.

PETERSON, R. and BERGER, D. (1975) 'Cycles in symbol production: The case of popular music', *American Sociological Review*, **40**, pp. 158–73.

PETHIA, R. (1983) *Pseudo-History in Management Textbooks: Illustrations and Comments*, Working Paper Series, Vol. II, No. 4, Bowling Green, KY: Kentucky College of Business Administration, Western Kentucky University.

PFEFFER, J. (1981) *Power in Organizations*, Boston: Pitman.

PHYSICS SURVEY COMMITTEE, NATIONAL RESEARCH COUNCIL (1972) *Physics in Perspective, Vol. 1*, Washington, DC: National Academy of Sciences.

PIERSON, F.C. *et al.* (1959) *The Education of American Businessmen*, New York: McGraw-Hill.

PORTER, B. and CZUJKO, R. (1986) 'Becoming a professional physicist: A statistical overview', *Physics Today*, **39**(6), pp. 70–8.

POSTER, M. (1990) *The Mode of Information: Poststructuralism and Social Context*, Chicago: The University of Chicago Press.

POWELL, W. (1990) 'Neither market nor hierarchy: Networks forms of organization', *Research in Organizational Behavior*, **12**, pp. 295–336.

RAIZEN, S. and JONES, L. (1985) *Indicators of Precollege Education in Science and Mathematics*, Washington, DC: National Academy Press.

RAMSDEN, P. and ENTWISTLE, N. (1981) 'Effects of academic departments on students' approaches to studying', *British Journal of Educational Psychology*, **51**, pp. 368–83.

ROSALDO, R. (1989) *Culture and Truth: The Remaking of Social Analysis*, Boston: Beacon Press.

ROSE, D. (1987) *Black American Street Life: South Philadelphia, 1969–1971*, Philadelphia: University of Pennsylvania Press.

SALJO, R. (1981) 'Learning approach and outcome: Some empirical observations', *Instructional Science*, **10**, pp. 47–65.

SALJO, R. and WYNDHAMN, J. (1990) 'Problem-solving, academic performance and situated reasoning: A study of joint cognitive activity in the formal setting', *British Journal of Educational Psychology*, **60**, pp. 245–54.

SAUNDERS, F. (1936) *A Survey of Physics for College Students*, New York: Henry Holt and Company.

SCHWARTZ COWAN, R. (1987) 'The consumption junction: A proposal for research strategies in the sociology of technology', in BIJKER, W., HUGHES, T. and PINCH, T. (Eds) *The Social Construction of Technological Systems*, Cambridge, MA: The MIT Press, pp. 261–80.

SMAIL, B. (1987) 'Organizing the curriculum to fit girls' interests', in KELLY, A. (Ed.) *Science for Girls?*, Milton Keynes: Open University Press, pp. 80–8.

SMITH, D. (1987) *The Everyday World as Problematic*, Boston: Northeastern University Press.

SOJA, E. (1985) 'The spatiality of social life: Towards a transformative retheorisation', in GREGORY, D. and URRY, J. (Eds) *Social Relations and Spatial Relations*, New York: St Martin's Press, pp. 90–127.

SOJA, E. (1989) *Postmodern Geographies: The Reassertion of Space in Critical Social Theory*, London: Verso.

References

SPAIN, D. (1992) *Gendered Spaces*, Chapel Hill: The University of North Carolina Press.

SPRINGBETT, B. (1958) 'Factors affecting the final decision in the employment interview', *Canadian Journal of Psychology*, **12**, pp. 13–22.

STEWART, M. and FAUX, M. (1979) *Executive Etiquette: How to Make Your Way to the Top with Grace and Style*, New York: St Martin's Press.

SUCHMAN, L. (1987) *Plans and Situated Actions: The Problem of Human/Machine Communication*, Cambridge: Cambridge University Press.

SWEET, W. (1988) 'AIP releases first major survey of high school physics teachers', *Physics Today*, **41**(11), pp. 93–4.

TIPLER, P. (1969) *Foundations of Modern Physics*, New York: Worth Publishers.

TRAWEEK, S. (1988) *Beamtimes and Lifetimes: The World of High Energy Physicists*, Cambridge, MA: Harvard University Press.

USEEM, M. (1986) 'What the research shows', in JOHNSTON, J.S., Jr. *et al. Educating Managers*, San Francisco: Jossey-Bass, pp. 70–101.

VYGOTSKY, L. (1978) *Mind in Society: The Development of Higher Psychological Processes* (Edited by COLE, M., JOHN-STEINER, V., SCRIBNER, S. and SOUBERMAN, E.), Cambridge, MA: Harvard University Press.

VYGOTSKY, L. (1986) *Thought and Language* (Edited by KOZULIN, A.), Cambridge, MA: MIT Press.

WELLMAN, B. (1983) 'Network analysis: Some principles', in COLLINS, R. (Ed.) *Sociological Theory, 1983*, San Francisco: Jossey-Bass, pp. 155–200.

WERTS, C. (1973) 'Social class and initial career choice of college freshmen', in EIDUSON, B. and BECKMAN, L. (Eds) *Science as a Career Choice*, New York: Russell Sage, pp. 75–81.

WERTSCH, J. (1986) *Vygotsky and the Social Formation of Mind*, Cambridge, MA: Harvard University Press.

WHEELER, J. (1966) 'The development of AACSB Standards', in AMERICAN ASSOCIATION OF COLLEGIATE SCHOOLS OF BUSINESS, *The American Association of Collegiate Schools of Business 1916–1966*, Homewood, IL: Richard D. Irwin, pp. 19–83.

WHITE, S. and SIEGEL, A. (1984) 'Cognitive development in time and space', in ROGOFF, B. and LAVE, J. (Eds) *Everyday Cognition: Its Development in Social Context*, Cambridge, MA: Harvard University Press, pp. 238–77.

WHITLEY, R. (1984) *The Intellectual and Social Organization of the Sciences*, Oxford: Clarendon Press.

WILLIAMS, R. (1977) *Marxism and Literature*, London: Oxford University Press.

WILLIS, P. (1981) *Learning to Labor*, New York: Columbia University Press.

WOOLGAR, S. (1987) 'Reconstructing man and machine: A note on sociological critiques of cognitivism', in BIJKER, W., HUGHES, T. and PINCH, T. (Eds) *The Social Construction of Technological Systems*, Cambridge, MA: The MIT Press, pp. 311–28.

WOOLGAR, S. (1988) *Science: The Very Idea*, Chichester: Ellis Horwood Limited.

Index